There

Hitler's Gift to the Jews

Norbert Troller

Translated by
Susan E. Cernyak-Spatz

Edited by Joel Shatzky

With the assistance of Richard Ives
and Doris Rauch

sienstadt

The University of North Carolina Press

Chapel Hill & London

Library of Congress Cataloging-in-Publication Data
Troller, Norbert.
Theresienstadt : Hitler's gift to the Jews / by Norbert Troller ;
translated by Susan E. Cernyak-Spatz ; edited by Joel
Shatzky with the assistance of Richard Ives and Doris Rauch.
p. cm.
Translation of an untitled manuscript.
Includes bibliographical references and index.
ISBN 0-8078-1965-4 (cloth : alk. paper)
ISBN 0-8078-5584-7 (pbk.: alk. paper)
1. Terezin (Czechoslovakia : Concentration camp).
2. Troller, Norbert. 3. Holocaust, Jewish (1939–1945)—
Czechoslovakia—Personal narratives. 4. Prisoners of war as
artists. I. Shatzky, Joel. II. Ives, Richard, 1925–
III. Rauch, Doris. IV. Title.
D805.C9T76 1991
940.53'174371—dc20
90-47029
CIP

Manufactured in the United States of America
cloth : 08 07 06 05 04   5 4 3 2 1
paper : 08 07 06 05 04   5 4 3 2 1

Frontispiece: Portrait of Norbert Troller.
(Courtesy Yeshiva University Museum)

THIS BOOK WAS DIGITALLY PRINTED.

A few days before the end of World War II, I was lucky enough to be among several thousands of concentration camp inmates rescued from Germany to Sweden by Count Folke Bernadotte and the International Red Cross. We were recuperating in the countryside when I learned from another ex-prisoner that my beloved uncle Noriček had been among the artists of Terezín who were arrested and imprisoned in the notorious Kleine Festung, from which no one ever had emerged alive. I had last seen him on September 1, 1942, when my mother—his favorite sister—and I left Terezín in a transport to the East whose destination turned out to be Estonia.

As soon as communications between Sweden and Czechoslovakia had been established, I wired a friend in Brno to let her know that I was alive and to inquire about other family members she might have heard from. Convinced that he had perished, I did not ask about Noriček. To this day I burst into tears when I recall the moment in the Swedish Boy Scout home in Värnamo when a telephone operator read to me an English telegram from Brno signed, "Your happiest uncle Norbert Troller."

Noriček had been my favorite uncle when I was growing up in Brno, and we developed a very close and loving relationship when we were the only ones of the Troller family to surface alive from the vortex of the concentration camps. Many were the hours here in the United States I listened spellbound to the stories he told of his adventures before, after, but especially during the war. He was a raconteur par excellence and loved life—even the worst of it! I am glad that he was granted the time to write about it and grateful to Susan and Joel for their loving labor in translating and editing his Terezín memoir.

Doris Rauch
Washington, D.C.
May 17, 1990

CONTENTS

Foreword by Sylvia Axelrod Herskovitz, xi

Acknowledgments, xiii

A Note on the Translation, xv

Editor's Note, xvii

Introduction, xix

Chapter 1. Warning Signs, 1

Chapter 2. Expulsion, Transports, and Entering the Camp, 7

Chapter 3. Theresienstadt, 20

Chapter 4. "Protection," 33

Chapter 5. The Transports, 46

Chapter 6. Rations and the Schleuse, 52

Chapter 7. The Fate of My Family, 60

Chapter 8. Life in the Ghetto, 70

Chapter 9. Love and Sex in Theresienstadt, 89

Chapter 10. A Taste of Freedom, 103

Chapter 11. "Kumbalistics," 111

Chapter 12. The Eternal Romantic, 117

Chapter 13. The "Painters' Affair," 131

Chapter 14. A Convict in the Little Fortress, 143

Notes, 161

Glossary, 175

Index, 179

ILLUSTRATIONS

Portrait of Norbert Troller, Frontispiece

Waiting for transport, 14

View of the church steeple, 18

Death cart, 24

Cemetery, 29

Zucker's kumbal, 43

Hohenelbe park, 48

Elderly person climbing to attic quarters, 54

Man in the schleuse, 57

Sudeten barracks: three-tiered bunks, 72

Line-up for food, 73

Dresdner barracks courtyard, 74

Courtyard concert: audience, 75

Courtyard concert: performers, 76

Magdeburger barracks main gate, 79

Ghetto bakery, 81

"Jedermann" ("Everyman") performance, 82

Inner court, 84

Little courtyard, 85

"Bubi" Windholz, 101

Town of Leitmeritz, 105

Ramparts, 106

Mill, 107

Smithy, 109

Kumbals, 114

Troller's sketch of the SS mess hall with "Jewish" candelabra

crossed out, 116

Hohenelbe hospital ward, 129

Little Fortress, 145

FOREWORD

It is now more than eleven years since Norbert Troller first walked into my office and told me that he had been a prisoner in Terezin and had secretly drawn life inside the ghetto.

When he told me the almost miraculous way in which his pictures were saved and retrieved after the war, I knew that we wanted to give him an exhibition. Since Norbert was already in his eighties, we did not have the luxury of time. He had been painstakingly writing his memoirs, and these served as the basis for the essays accompanying the drawings.

Throughout the preparation of the exhibition, Norbert worked with us very closely and came innumerable times to the museum from his apartment in the East 70s. He was so happy that his work was at last being shown and his sentiments given public recognition. All his life he had been a modest and unassuming person who never quite believed that his work could be considered art, since he thought of himself as architect rather than artist.

When it came to designing the installation, he made numerous sketches indicating how the chairs were to be arranged in the exhibition hall because he was so concerned that everything should be perfect. What a thrill it was for him to come to the opening and see his friends of the past forty years. His former boss at Federation, the National Jewish Welfare Board when Troller was first employed there, Sanford Solender, spoke a few words and said that he was surprised to find out that Norbert was an artist as well as an architect. During the entire time that Troller worked at Federation designing Jewish community centers and synagogues across the United States, he had never told anyone of his hidden pictures.

I am delighted that at long last Norbert Troller is the subject of a fine book. To have his work published was his ultimate ambition, and I am happy that Yeshiva University Museum was able to initiate the exhibition and catalog that first brought him to public attention.

It was very sad when Norbert passed away a few months after the exhibition opened in 1981; it was still up at the time, and next to his portrait by Peter Kien, we posted his obituary. All of us were grateful that we had mounted the exhibition in his lifetime and had produced a catalog of which he was very proud. And I am especially thankful that we had all of the work photographed, thus preserving intact the record of a sensitive artistic human being who, in his own words, was a born survivor.

Sylvia Axelrod Herskovitz, Director
Yeshiva University Museum

ACKNOWLEDGMENTS

We wish to thank the Leo Baeck Institute and its staff for their help and advice to us while we were working with the Troller manuscript and pictures. We are especially appreciative of the efforts of Diane Spielmann and Jacqueline Rea, the institute's art curator. Sylvia Axelrod Herskovitz, the director of the Yeshiva University Museum, also provided us with valuable materials, particularly the collection of slides from the exhibition of Troller's work at the museum, which she compiled with Norbert Troller's assistance shortly before his death in 1981. The preface she wrote for the catalog to the Troller exhibition also provided us with valuable biographical information on Troller.

We are grateful to Sybil Milton for her helpful suggestions in the revision of the Introduction. Our colleagues on the library staffs both at the Cortland Memorial Library at the State University of New York, College at Cortland, and Atkins Library at the University of North Carolina at Charlotte also gave valuable assistance. Of special help in aiding in the research for the Introduction and the notes was Sanford Gutman of the history department at Cortland. Thanks as well are due to Morris Schappes, editor of Jewish Currents, Eberhard Alsen of the English department and Irmgard Taylor of the language department at Cortland for their advice on the translation, and to Vincent Minnella of the Sperry Center at Cortland for his invaluable help in formatting the text.

Finally, we wish to acknowledge, with deep appreciation, the generosity of George Stefan Troller, Herbert Trent, and Doris Rauch in supporting the publication of their uncle's memoirs and pictures.

Joel Shatzky
Susan E. Cernyak-Spatz

A NOTE ON THE TRANSLATION

Norbert Troller grew up at the turn of the century in that German-speaking area of the Austro-Hungarian Empire that was to become part of Czechoslovakia; it included Böhmen, Mähren, and die Slovakei. The Jews of his generation, though inordinately proud of and loyal to the young Czechoslovakian Republic, still retained their German language and culture.

Their German had a peculiar flavor that in literary circles had acquired the epithet "Prager Deutsch." Therefore, the translation has been prepared with this fact in mind. I have tried to retain as much of that flavor as colloquial but correct English would allow.

Many sentences in the original manuscript were almost lapidary, lacking verbs or using verbal nouns, which is a peculiarity of "Prager Deutsch." In those cases I have completed the sentence according to the apparent intentions of the author. When there was no available English equivalent for an idiom, I have tried to substitute the closest colloquial English meaning. Most idioms had their cognate equivalents in English.

It becomes clear, even in the translated version, that the Czech Jews used both German and Czech interchangeably. For example, Troller uses the Czech word šlupky, meaning "potato peels," instead of its German equivalent.

The publisher has romanized and lowercased German nouns, treating them in a manner consistent with English nouns, in order to avoid the visual repetition of italic interruption throughout the English text.

Joel Shatzky and I have attempted to bring the story of Theresienstadt, so long overlooked in the body of Holocaust memoirs, to the attention of the public. Our collaboration has been enriching for me; and I hope that the end product will fulfill the purpose of commemorating Norbert Troller and the lives of the people he so vividly describes in his words and pictures.

Susan E. Cernyak-Spatz

EDITOR'S NOTE

In preparing these memoirs, the editor used punctuation that would aid the reader as much as possible in understanding the text. Troller's narrative took several years to compose, he sometimes wrote additional segments without having access to earlier ones, and he did not edit his writings before his death. As a result, some sections of the narrative were quite repetitive and have been omitted. Ellipses are used to indicate such omissions.

Within the memoirs, parentheses ( ) indicate Troller's own parenthetical remarks. Brackets [ ] are used for interpolations of Troller's words that were originally in one section of the narrative and were moved to another by the editor. Interpolations are identified in the notes by the pagination of the original manuscript in Troller's own handwriting, which is housed in the Leo Baeck Institute. The translator's and the editor's additions are enclosed in curly brackets { }.

The present manuscript is a portion of a larger narrative that Troller wrote in German. It began with his childhood, included his experiences in Theresienstadt, and continued when he was deported to Auschwitz. The editor and translator felt, however, that since these other portions of the narrative were not relevant to Troller's experiences in Theresienstadt, they should not be included in the present volume. The sketches and watercolors accompanying the text, moreover, were rendered by Troller exclusively while he was in Theresienstadt. Thus, they are appropriate only to that portion of the narrative.

Although Troller made over 300 drawings and watercolors while in Theresienstadt, the costs of reproducing them and the difficulties of integrating them into the text would make it impossible to replicate all of them in this volume. A number of the most vivid works, however, several of which appeared in the Yeshiva University Museum catalog when Troller's work was exhibited there in 1981, are included.

Wherever possible, the persons mentioned by Troller are identified. A number of them, however, particularly personal friends, could not be traced.

Finally, Troller often switches tenses in the narrative, especially into the present from the past in order to dramatize particular scenes. Where they appear to be logically and effectively employed, these tense shifts have been retained; however, tenses have occasionally been altered for the sake of consistency.

Joel Shatzky

INTRODUCTION

Even if we could understand the nature of evil, it is difficult to imagine the source of the terrifying logic by which the Nazis waged their war of extermination against the Jews of Europe. In that brief period between 1939 and 1945, one thousand years of religion, culture, and tradition were ground almost into oblivion. It is even more difficult to conceive a scale upon which we could weigh the many outrages committed by the Third Reich against humanity. Whether through the legalisms that perverted the notion of justice in the Nuremberg Laws, the horrors of the pogrom in Germany in 1938 (popularly known as Kristallnacht), the atrocities of the death squads in Eastern Europe and the Soviet Union, or the grim "logic" embodied in the "Final Solution" itself, we cannot help but see a pattern, a plan of action, a system that the Nazis developed, modified, and attempted to perfect in order to destroy an entire people.

Even after all was lost, the Allies being in command of the air and closing in from east and west, the leadership of the Third Reich continued its efforts to make Europe Judenrein (Jew-free), as if that hideous "achievement" could serve as a lasting monument to Hitler. Raul Hilberg's comprehensive study, The Destruction of the European Jews,[1] gives one a sense of the scope of this enterprise of genocide. The list of the names of the extermination centers will remain in our memories forever: Treblinka, Bełżec, Auschwitz-Birkenau, Sobibor, Chełmno, Majdanek. Yet, it is the insane logic of the Nazis' plan that while they were isolating the Jews from the rest of the populations of Europe, while they were murdering them in every conceivable way—shootings, gassings, starvation, disease—the leadership really thought they could keep the "Final Solution" a secret from the rest of the world. One of the worst taunts thrown at their Jewish victims by the Nazi guards in the camps was that "no one would believe" that the organized destruction of the Jews of Europe had ever taken place; they would just "vanish," and the civilized world would never discover how.

If one could allow the word "success" to be attached to the Nazis' madness, then surely their deception of their victims was their greatest success. But their ability to deceive so many people reveals less about their ingenuity than it shows that infinite capacity for hope that the Jews clung to even as they were being driven into the extermination camps.

Thus, ironically, hope was the most effective weapon the Nazis used against their victims even as, at every turn, the Jews' reasons for having any hope that they could survive their tormentors vanished. Those who resisted heroically, those who fought with nothing more than courage and a few weapons against the most highly trained and best equipped army in the world at that time, have had their stories told.[2] Most of the Jews who were murdered in the camps of Poland went to their deaths, however, without active resistance, holding on to some slim hope that their murderers were still the humane, civilized people the world had long believed them to be.

In fact, the Nazis wanted to encourage that idea of their civility so that even if defeat should come, their deeds would remain unknown. Not only did they expend great effort to conceal the "Final Solution," but they attempted to create a colossal hoax: that rather than being tortured and killed, the Jews of Europe were actually well-treated "guests" of the Third Reich. Thus, high on the list of Nazi crimes is the ghetto in which they tried to deceive those who would later judge them; the ghetto to which they invited the Red Cross to show how "humane" they were to the Jews; the ghetto in which the perversion of truth became the normal way of conducting business: Ghetto Theresienstadt.

THERESIENSTADT

Originally a garrison town founded in 1780 by the Emperor Joseph II in honor of his mother, the Empress Maria Theresa, Theresienstadt was converted into a "model" ghetto with the arrival of the first Jewish prisoners on November 24, 1941. The ghetto, during the deportations of German Jews, was used as an excuse for the deportation of elderly Jews who, plainly, could not have been of any use in doing forced labor in the East where the extermination camps were located. With this logic, when the deportations of Central European Jews to the killing centers began in the spring of 1942, certain groups were excluded, many of whom were in Theresienstadt: invalids, those over sixty-five, decorated and disabled war veterans, those in mixed marriages and their children, and prominent Jews, prominenten, who had connections.[3] The remainder of the Jews from the German-speaking areas of the Reich—Austria and Germany—who were to be "rewarded" by being sent to Theresienstadt found themselves trapped in what was really a collection point for Jews from Czechoslovakia, Hungary, Luxembourg, the Netherlands, and Denmark as well as the Reich itself. They would be misled by the apparently less harsh conditions in the ghetto, dispossessed of all they owned, and then sent to their deaths in "the East."

Although the mortality rate does not compare with those of the worst of the camps in Poland, the statistics for Theresienstadt are terrible in themselves. Of the 140,000 people who entered this walled town between November 1941 and April 1945, one month before the Russian army arrived and liberated it, almost 90,000 were sent to their deaths in Auschwitz-Birkenau, Treblinka, and several lesser-known camps; another 33,000 died in the ghetto itself, most from hunger and disease, many of these elderly people and children; and only 16,832 survived, many of whom entered near the end of the war when living conditions had improved and the deportations had practically stopped. These figures are even more perverse if one realizes that Theresienstadt was considered to be a model ghetto by the Nazi hierarchy, in which only the "privileged" German and other German-speaking Jews were sent so as to assure some of the more sympathetic Germans that their comrades, particularly veterans of World War I, would be better treated than their "inferior" coreligionists who lived in the Slavic countries. Those incarcerated in Theresienstadt included a number of well-known artists, musicians, scholars, judges, and other members of the cream of the social and intellectual world of pre-Hitler Germany. Such figures as Heinrich Mann's first wife and the conductor, Karel Ancerl, were among those who suffered the cruelties of this overcrowded, disease-ridden place that the Nazis dubbed "self-governing," complete with an *Ältestenrat* (Council of Elders), an elaborate bureaucracy, "shops," and even a "bank" that issued worthless currency picturing Moses holding the Ten Commandments!

All of this, of course, was a front to conceal the terrible conditions under which the inmates of the ghetto were living and dying. For despite the fact that the Nazis felt so secure in their subterfuge that they even invited the Red Cross to inspect Theresienstadt twice before the end of the war, the ghetto was only different in the most superficial way from the worst of the others. They all served one purpose: to kill off as many Jews as quickly and efficiently as possible.

The practices of the Nazis in Theresienstadt, which created the impression that the Jews were being well treated, were similar to later deceptions in other camps. The Nazis developed a facade of the kindly face masking the death's head to lull the victims into a false sense of security by creating the impression that the changing rooms adjacent to the gas chambers in which the innocent victims would be killed were to lead them into showers for delousing. The methodology used to develop these deceptions can be most clearly seen in Theresienstadt where, although the victims were never murdered outright,[4] they were placed into such conditions that their survival over any long period of time, particularly if they were elderly, was highly unlikely. Yet the facade was effective enough apparently to fool the Red Cross when they reported the results of their inspection of the ghetto in June 1944. The extent of the hoax can be best appreciated if one were to view the still-surviving film, *Der Führer schenkt den Juden eine Stadt* ("The Führer Grants a City to the Jews") in which inmates were depicted as well-fed, well-dressed "guests" of the Reich, occupying their time with gentle conversation and cultural activities while waiting out the war as "typical" inmates of the Reich's "resettlement camps."

H. G. Adler describes what he sees as the inherent relationship between Theresienstadt and Auschwitz as different forms of a "game":

> In Auschwitz, there was only the naked despair or the pitiless recognition of the game, and even if there existed a spark of an indestructible vitality, even if the soul managed to escape from time to time into a delusion, in the long run no one could deceive himself, everyone had to look reality in the face.
>
> It was different in Theresienstadt. Everything there could be pushed aside, illusion flourished wildly, and hope, only mildly dampened by anxiety would eclipse everything that was hidden under an impenetrable haze. Nowhere had the inmates of a camp pushed the

true face of the period further into an unknown future than here. . . .
Only occasionally would the truth arise from the depths, touch the
inmates, and after a bit of fright, they would [go back] into their existence of masks of masks.[5]

It was this movie-set atmosphere to which the Danish Red Cross was
invited on June 23, 1944. Months in preparation, the "Embellishment," as
it was called, included the deportation of more than 5,000 of the inmates
to the East shortly before the inspection of the ghetto so that Theresienstadt would not appear to be overcrowded. Although the Red Cross was
not entirely taken in by the Nazis' hoax, Dr. Franz Hvass, head of the
Danish delegation, reported, "I cannot but express my admiration, which
one must have for the Jewish people, who through their unique dedica-
tion have managed within the frame of the self-administration to create
such relatively good living conditions for their fellow Jews."[46]

The ghetto was set up to foster these false impressions since, as already
mentioned, many of the inmates were artists, musicians, and other cultural and intellectual leaders of the Jewish community. The variety of activities "permitted" in the ghetto included concerts, opera performances, and
lectures, which created the false perception of a sense of freedom in the
minds of the inmates. The translator of this memoir, Dr. Susan E. Cernyak-Spatz, describes her own experiences while a prisoner in Theresienstadt: "The older ghetto inhabitants found consolation and uplift in the
cultural activities, which helped them to forget temporarily their dreary
present. For the young people, it provided a source of strength, mental
discipline, and courage."[7] In this way, both objectives of the Nazis were
fulfilled: the ghetto served their goal of reducing the Jewish population
through malnutrition, disease, and deportations, and yet an atmosphere
was created in which their true purpose was concealed both from those

who were invited to inspect the ghetto and, although to a lesser extent, from the Jews themselves.

Ghetto Theresienstadt was established in November 1941 by the first head of Reich Security, Reinhold Heydrich, who appointed Siegfried Seidl in the following month to be the first commandant of the ghetto. Seidl was a sadistic man who ordered the only executions actually carried out within the walls of the ghetto early in 1942 and frequently resorted to beatings of the inmates. On Adolf Eichmann's orders, he was dismissed in June 1943 because he was not in sufficient sympathy with the purposes of the ghetto which was now to be used as a showplace, a "ghetto for old people," the "pensioner's home" for those Jews from the Reich who were being "rewarded" for their past service to their country by being settled there. Anton Burger, Seidl's successor, administered the ghetto until February 1944. It was during his rule that the first of the three Judenältester (heads of the Council of Elders), Jakob Edelstein, who acted as the leader of the Jewish community but was subject to the orders of the SS, was deported with 5,000 of his fellow Czechs in December 1943 to the East. His successor, Paul Eppstein, was murdered by the Nazis in September 1944 and was replaced by Benjamin Murmelstein who survived the war. It was during Burger's tenure as well that 200–300 Jews lost their lives in a single night on November 11, 1943, during a "census count" in which all 40,000 inmates of the ghetto were forced to stand in a field all night. Burger was succeeded by Karl Rahm who administered the "Embellishment" in order to attempt to deceive the Red Cross Commission. It was not until the war was only several months from ending that the deportation of Jews from Theresienstadt to the death camps finally ceased and less than two months before the ghetto was liberated on May 5, 1945, that transports bringing new victims were halted. It was to Theresienstadt that Norbert Troller came only several months after it was established.

NORBERT TROLLER

Norbert Troller was born in 1896 in Brünn (Brno), Austro-Hungary, the youngest of five children. In 1915, after completing his high school education, he volunteered for service in the Austrian army, serving for four years in the Alpine Light Infantry and Mountain Artillery. After being released from a prisoner-of-war camp in Italy in 1919, Troller attended architectural school in Brünn, graduating in 1925, and moved to Vienna where he completed his studies at the Academy of Fine Arts in 1927. Although initially set back by the depression in Europe several years later, Troller opened an office in Brünn where his architectural practice flourished until 1939 when Czechoslovakia fell to the Nazis.

His home and practice "expropriated" by the Germans, Troller was sent to Theresienstadt in March 1942 where he remained until September 1944, when he was transported to Auschwitz for his part in what has been called the "Painters' Affair," in which he and several of his fellow artists were surreptitiously depicting the desperate lives of the inmates of Theresienstadt. When some of these pictures were smuggled out and photos of them subsequently appeared in the Swiss press, an investigation ensued and Troller was caught along with a number of more prominent artists. The entire matter is described by Troller in his memoir. Liberated by the Russians from Auschwitz in January 1945, Troller returned to Brünn to begin a new life. He remained in his native town, helping to rebuild his family's fur business as well as his own architectural practice until 1948, when, after the Communists took over Czechoslovakia, he was able to emigrate to the United States.

He was hired, shortly after his arrival in this country in September 1948, as an architect with the National Jewish Welfare Board. In his ten years with the organization, he designed sixty synagogues, then set up his own company in 1959, which he ran until his retirement in 1978.

During his career, Troller won a number of awards and competitions for his architectural designs in both Czechoslovakia and the United States. From May 1981 through April 1982 Yeshiva University Museum exhibited a selection of his drawings and watercolors of Theresienstadt: "Terezín 1942–1945 through the Eyes of Norbert Troller." Troller had completed a draft of his memoirs at the time of his death, which occurred during the exhibition.[8]

A sketch Mr. Troller made of his family tree reveals the devastation suffered by his relatives at the hands of the Nazis. His brother Ernst and sisters Ida and Alice died in concentration camps, the former two along with their spouses. Two of Ernst's sons, Ludwig and Fritz, as well as Ida's daughters, Hanne and Marianne, perished with their parents. Only Troller's brother Karl and his family were able to escape from Europe.

After the Anschluss, Karl, his wife, and his son George escaped from Brünn via Italy and southern France and took the last ship from Portugal to the United States, aided by an affidavit sent by an American friend, Joe Wantoch. Karl's older son, Herbert, escaped to England via Brussels. Karl returned to Vienna in 1958 and died near there in 1974 at the age of ninety-one. (George Troller, the younger son, subsequently wrote a trilogy of screenplays that paralleled his experiences during his escape that have been successfully produced as "God Doesn't Remember Us Anymore," "Santa Fe," and "Welcome in Vienna." The films debuted in the United States in 1988.) The toll of those family members who died is summed up in the dying leaves of Troller's family tree: twelve of nineteen of his family's children and seven of twenty-eight of their grandchildren.

The diversity of places in which members of the Troller family either died or were incarcerated is indicative of the elaborate system developed by the Nazis to exterminate the Jews. Troller, along with his sister Alice, her daughter Doris (Troller uses her German name, Dora), and his brother Ernst and sister Ida Bunzl-Federn and their families, were all transported to Theresienstadt at approximately the same time in early 1942. It was at this time that the Nazis were systematically "cleaning out" the Jewish populations of Germany, Austria, and the *Protektorat*, their designation for the German-occupied area of Czechoslovakia: Bohemia and Moravia. These Jews were deported to Theresienstadt. Subsequently, most of those who survived the starvation diet and poor sanitary conditions of Theresienstadt—and several of Troller's family did not—were sent to Auschwitz-Birkenau. A cousin, Paul, and his family were sent directly to the Łódź ghetto in Poland, where they perished. Besides Troller himself, the only other family member who survived the Holocaust in Europe was his niece, Doris, whose mother was murdered in a work camp in Estonia because she was—according to Doris—"overage" while Doris lived through the rigors of the camp and was finally liberated. Each of these relative's stories is, in itself, heartbreaking.

Although already in possession of a visa for England, his cousin Paul, in an effort to save his stepson from deportation, made the mistake of trying to appeal to the Gestapo, which resulted in his entire family, his wife and three children, being sent to Łódź. Troller's brother Ernst and his family met as cruel a fate when one of his sons, Ludwig, was denounced for *rassenschande* (miscegenation) by the jilted suitor of a Czech girl he had been courting. As a result, the entire family was transported to Theresienstadt. Of the three sons, only Hans, the youngest, escaped. He emigrated to Huddersfield, England, in 1939 and settled in California after the war where he committed suicide in the late 1960s.

Troller poignantly describes the death of his elderly brother-in-law, Julius Bunzl-Federn, his sister Ida's husband, when he meets him in the ghetto:

> He was a composer and virtuoso manqué, who played the piano enchantingly. He was completely unworldly but had to pursue a com-

mercial career, for which he had neither talent, inclination, nor training. . . . He invented a "musical notation typewriter" to record his and
other so-called composers' works. . . . Another . . . "expert" produced
some mechanical blueprints. The blueprints apparently remained Julius's idée fixe for the rest of his life. . . . He already was quite old
when he arrived in Theresienstadt. . . ; his beard had turned white.
Like most old people in Theresienstadt he soon contracted enteritis,
the form of diarrhea frequently deadly for the elderly. He was moved
into one of the block sickrooms, where I visited him. He was so
weak, so emaciated, obviously dying, his beard untrimmed. He asked
me to remove a packet of papers from under his pillow. I opened it—
it contained the blueprints of his cloud cuckooland musical notation
typewriter. "Guard them well, my life's work is in them. I know that
one day the plans will become reality, only I shall not see it anymore."
Two days later he was dead.

But most moving is the description Troller gives of his feelings when he
discovers, while still in Brünn, that his widowed sister, Alice, and her
daughter, Doris, have been notified that they are to be deported. They
were among the first of his relatives to be sent off in December 1941 to
Theresienstadt.

Alice and her husband, Artur, who unfortunately died of cancer at
much too early an age, were my closest relatives and friends. . . . How
could I forget her constant comfort and sympathy, her devoted affection to a brother who so frequently strayed and got involved in
thoughtless affairs? How could I forget her caring and encouragement, and most of all her humor and wisdom? It was unbearable
torture to have to accompany Alice and her little Dora, our Dora, to
the impending deportation, to have to suppress tears, find words of
comfort, when I myself was brokenhearted and in need of consola-

tion. To part from the dearest of our friends, to see them disappear into the unknown, could only be compared to a farewell at the gates of the Underworld. Devastated, heartbroken, I finally reached my home after wandering around aimlessly.

Troller was to meet his sister and niece months later in Theresienstadt where he attempted to put them under his "protection." He was unable to save them, and they were deported to Raasiku, Estonia, in September 1942. Alice was immediately taken away to be shot while Doris managed to survive, first in a political prison in Reval (Tallinn), and then in various camps in Estonia. Then she was shipped back to Germany where she worked in a munitions factory in Hamburg-Ochsenzoll. After a short time in Bergen-Belsen, she managed to get into a work detail and was finally ransomed with several thousand other prisoners to Sweden, arriving on May 1, 1945, the ransom having been arranged through Himmler by Count Folke Bernadotte.

Thus, the odyssey of many of Troller's relatives, most ending in death, is woven through his own narrative. It is a story filled with the tragedy of an era in which practically no one, if he or she had the misfortune of being a Jew, no matter how wealthy, talented, or well connected, would find any mercy from the pitiless, faceless, malevolence of the Nazi death machine.

As striking as the narrative itself are the sketches and watercolors that Troller was able to render of the life of quiet desperation led by the inmates of the ghetto. Literally under the noses of the Nazis, Troller methodically and bravely drew on scraps of paper and sketching sheets stolen from the architectural department where he worked the daily life of the ghetto: the bakery, the hospital, the crowds at various cultural events, the vaulted rooms, the battlements and walls of the fortress town, and faces, faces, faces—a living record of those who would disappear into the transports to the East and those who died of disease and hunger in the ghetto itself. It was through the help of the sketches that Troller was able to recall his experiences in Theresienstadt. For it is this unique combination of words and pictures that gives this book its special place in the canon of eyewitness accounts of the Holocaust.

From his first words describing the day when the notices for deportation were slipped under the doors of the Jews of Brünn, Troller's memoir records, more than anything else, the feelings of hope, faith, and self-deception to which the victims clung as their only solace in a world gone mad. He writes, "Human nature has a tendency to be optimistic; we try to interpret the misfortunes of foreigners in such a way that we believe misfortune will pass us by because we were special cases." In contrast, the narrator reveals the stark terror of the Nazi roundup of their victims as they were being driven to the railway station and their unknown destination:

> Around midnight the yelling of the SS, barked commands: "*Raus, raus,* line up by floors." We get up, line up, with rucksack, tool kit, carryall, canteen filled with water; screaming children pull their mothers this way and that; we move downstairs, line up in rows of four and move out of the gate. It is completely dark; the oval driveway is lined with torches stuck into the ground, SS men standing between the torches to make sure no one escapes.

On his approach to Theresienstadt, the keen eye of the artist becomes evident when Troller, as if almost detached from the ominous situation in which he finds himself, describes his surroundings as he enters the ghetto:

> From a bird's-eye view Theresienstadt looked like an eight-pointed, elongated star. The sharp corners were formed by the entrenchments and the casemates; between them lay the deep moats now covered

with gardens, meadows, and fields, then the grass-covered ramparts, following the same star design, and inside of this star nestled the typical fortress-cum-garrison town, with militarily aligned roadways, no nooks or crannies, square blocks of houses, five vertical streets, and [twelve cross streets {which} formed the simple street grid].

One of the most intriguing portions of the narrative, however, is Troller's explanation of the system of "protection" that was used in Theresienstadt to prevent the relatives, friends, and colleagues of those Jews fortunate enough to be placed in positions of some influence in the ghetto from being deported on one of those endless transports to the East and certain death. The agony of conscience that those survivors had to endure while others were sent off is one of the most sensitive and problematic issues with which survivors of the Holocaust have to deal to this day.

In the beginning, I assumed rather naively that the SS issued the orders and made the selection as they had done in Brünn when they sent us to Theresienstadt. That was not the case here. With devilish baseness and cunning they did dictate the number of victims to be sent east, but they put the burden of selection on the Jews themselves; to select their own coreligionists, relatives, their friends. In the end this unbearable, desperate, cynical burden destroyed the community leaders who were forced to make the selections. The power over life and death forced on the Council of Elders was the main reason, the unavoidable force, behind the ever-increasing corruption in the ghetto; its single, solitary goal was life and "protection" from transports.

It is these and similar kinds of observations that make Norbert Troller's narrative of Theresienstadt unique in the literature describing this ghetto that the Nazis so carefully exploited near the end of the war to create a facade of humane treatment toward the Jews.

Troller's narrative ends at the time he was implicated, along with a half dozen other artists, in the "Painters' Affair" in July 1944. Arrested along with such well-known figures as Fritta, Otto Ungar, and Leo Haas, who had smuggled out some of their drawings revealing the real horrors of Theresienstadt, Troller chillingly describes the truly brutal nature of the Nazis behind the facade that they had tried to present when the Red Cross had visited the camp just a month before. Troller describes how he and his fellow "conspirators" were sent to the *Kleine Festung* (Little Fortress), the dreaded prison outside the walls of Theresienstadt that was mostly used for political prisoners. The contrast between life in the Ghetto Theresienstadt itself, hard as it was, and the conditions in the Little Fortress is so stark that it could be said that Troller experienced the best and the worst treatment that the Nazis could give him. Yet he was able to survive through it all.

Although the narrative in this book ends with his removal from the Little Fortress and the beginning of his journey to Auschwitz as a "political" prisoner (a designation that saved his life), Norbert Troller's fight for survival was to continue for several more months in which, once again, his ingenuity saved him from death. Arriving in Auschwitz in September 1944, he managed to convince a *kapo* that he would teach him architecture in exchange for food. The kapo provided the extra rations, and when Troller ran out of "lessons," he invented more until the camp was about to be evacuated in January 1945.

He then was able to evade the "death march" and left the camp with a friend, Karel Lagus, when the Nazis abandoned it. The two journeyed east to Cracow where they stayed in a monastery. Troller was able to supplement his meager diet at the monastery by going to some of the restaurants in Cracow and offering to paint scenic frescoes on the restaurant walls in exchange for food. Thus, he found a way to survive through the last months of the war. He then was able to reconstruct his life, rebuilding a prosperous business through his architectural practice in Brünn as well as his family's fur business.

Perhaps the most extraordinary circumstance in Troller's whole experience, however, occurred a year after the war was over. He had assumed that his drawings and watercolors of Theresienstadt had been destroyed by the Nazis as soon as he was arrested. Purely by the remotest chance, however, in June 1946, while on a visit to Prague, he happened to notice an elderly woman staring at him in the crowded streets. He asked who she was and discovered that she was Kathie Windholz, the wife of one of his old friends in Theresienstadt, whom he scarcely recognized. She explained that she and her husband, who had subsequently died in Auschwitz, had hidden Troller's sketches in a pillowcase in the rafters of his *kumbal* (cubbyhole) as soon as they had heard that he had been arrested. Had Troller not met with Kathie Windholz on that day, he would never have found his work. She was the only living person who could have known of the existence of the sketches and their location, and she was leaving Czechoslovakia the following day to settle with relatives in Argentina. It was just by the remotest chance that she happened to have been in Prague to get her exit visa on the same day that Troller was visiting.

Troller drove to Theresienstadt that next weekend and discovered that it had returned to "normal." He located the house in which he had lived, which was now a bakery as it had been originally. Its former owner, who had been dispossessed by the Nazis in 1942, was once more running his bakery as if nothing had happened in the intervening years.

Troller described his mounting excitement as he entered the bakery:

I . . . introduced myself and asked politely for permission to visit the attic, having lived there for such a long time during the Nazi period. The baker, a friendly Czech, agreed, handed me the attic key, and I went up the stairs. It was half-dark there, dusty, sooty, and I am sure populated by half a million fleas again, filled with new debris, new old broken-down furniture, lots of suitcases and trunks, shabby, thread-bare rolls of carpeting, chairs for invalids, etc. I quickly found a da-maged oak table, put it under the rafter with the "Coxbeam," put an empty trunk on the table, and climbed quickly and nimbly to reach {the rafter}. I put my hand in the gap of the firewall, and there it was— my treasure, wrapped in a pillowcase, invisible from the outside, now resting in my dirty, trembling hands. Hurrah![9]

Once the sketches were found, however, another thirty-five years passed before they were to be put on public display. Troller had felt that his artistic efforts were unworthy of any notice, but once he saw an exhibit of Holocaust art at the Yeshiva University Museum, he was inspired to pre-sent to officials there his own pictorial rendition of his experiences during the Holocaust.

These, as has been mentioned, were exhibited at the Yeshiva University Museum from May 1981 to April 1982. For several years previous to this, Troller was at work writing his memoirs, which remained unedited in manuscript at the time of his death in December 1981. They, along with the sketches and watercolors, were deposited in the Leo Baeck Institute in New York City by Doris Rauch, Troller's niece and executrix of his estate. It was at the Leo Baeck Institute that the editor and translator discovered this remarkable memoir and collection of drawings several years later.

With great courage Norbert Troller was able to write of his own feelings and experiences in a world of despair and fear. It was with even greater courage that he gambled again and again that the Nazis would not discover the visual record he was keeping of life in this "model" camp. It was his way of striking back at an enemy who had force and fear as his weapons but who lacked the intelligence to see that the "Final Solution" would be found out and revealed to all the world by those very victims whom the "Master Race" had regarded so contemptuously. That the memoirs and drawings of Norbert Troller have been preserved and can now be read and seen is this man's ultimate triumph over his tormentors, which even death cannot now deny him.

Joel Shatzky

THERESIENSTADT

1

WARNING SIGNS

The day came when the first Jewish immigrants among us were in imminent danger of deportation to the East. These immigrants were the Reichsdeutsch Jews {from the Reich} who had lived among us since 1933, and who unfortunately had not emigrated further west or east via Russia, Hungary, or Turkey. {Among them were} the Austrian Jews who had only arrived a short while ago {1938}. It was the Austrians who were the most insistent because they had learned from the experiences of the German Jews that the chances of finding a friendly country became more and more difficult, often impossible.[1] Among those anxious to leave was my brother Karl who had arrived in Brünn {Brno}, after having been imprisoned for a short time in Vienna, to join his wife Vilma and his son George who had preceded him to Brünn. Energetically, he made preparations to resume his journey, which after many difficulties and dangers, via Italy, France, and Portugal finally led him, successfully, to the United States.

The refugees who had remained {in Czechoslovakia} were simply summoned with hardly a chance to prepare themselves; {they were} driven together like a scattered herd of cattle, crammed into cattle cars, and transported to the East. Saying good-bye to them, many of whom had become dear friends, was all too heartbreaking for us to imagine.... Soon this farewell would be equally heartbreaking for us {when we were deported}.

We said good-bye to friends whom we had learned to love, and when they left we tried to delude ourselves with the thought: "These were German Jews from the Reich, after all—they are a special case and probably they will be resettled as German Jews somewhere in the east."[2] Human nature has a tendency to be optimistic; we try to interpret the misfortunes of foreigners in such a way that we believe misfortune will pass us by because we are special cases—in this instance citizens of the *Protektorat*, citizens of an occupied country—whom the Nazis would not dare to deport to the east because of international law, or for fear of offending international opinion. They did dare without considering "world opinion"—world opinion was blind, anyway, as far as the Jews were concerned, or at least it pretended not to know—and they did deport us to the east and to the "transit station," Terezin {Czech name for Theresienstadt}.

The first transports of German Jews from the Reich and Austrian Jews went directly to Minsk and the Lódź ghetto, renamed "Litzmannstadt" by the Nazis. Only a very few people found their way back after the war. It is said that little by little 98 percent of them were killed.

Here I must recall the victims of Łódź among my own family: My cousin, Paul Troller, his second wife {a native German}, and his two children from his first marriage {his first wife had died many years earlier} and a six-year-old stepson whose father had also been a German Jew from Leipzig. Because of these circumstances—the little boy's German birth—he was listed as a German emigrant in the Nazi transport lists. When the transports were assembled the boy received a summons to go on the transport alone without his despairing parents, a tragic, heartbreaking dilemma; all the more so because Paul already had a visa for England with an exit permit, but he had unfortunately waited too long to leave. Had he departed three days earlier, their security in the West would have been assured. Paul saw no other recourse but to go personally to the Gestapo headquarters in the Petschek Palais—the dreaded central office of all torture chambers and prisons in the Protektorat—to intervene on behalf of his stepson. The outcome of this intervention was that the Gestapo kept him there and ordered him to call his family to inform them that they would have to follow him immediately, regardless of the English visa and the exit permit. They were sent to Łódź, and of the five none came back.

If I interrupt the writing of these memoirs, it cannot be blamed on my being lazy or a paucity of ideas or memory. It is a kind of fear. Something in me, at this time, resists raising the unbearable, horrifying events of the past, reliving them again. My purpose, however, is not to trick myself and to forget, but to make sure the {events} are not forgotten, even if it means that barely healed wounds must be opened again.

Having survived the horrors, it is difficult to remember the frightful pressures to which one succumbed at a time when survival seemed impossible. It was a time when we were forced to make sudden decisions daily. There was no time to consider one's own feelings; there was only the constant pressure to act with lightning speed; no time to consider eventual pros and cons. One acted instinctively, spontaneously. The year

must have been 1941. We were still working as common laborers at the
railroad construction site in Maloměřice {suburb of Brünn}. We really believed that we would keep doing this kind of labor for the duration of the
war, and we hoped—unfortunately in vain—that nothing would change.

The first of the terrible blows that put an end to all our carefully nur-
tured optimism and all our hopes came in {autumn} 1941. It began with
vague rumors about transports in the near future. The rumors were persis-
tent enough to alert us and to cause us to think of making preparations,
just in case.

Everybody tried to store his remaining belongings with Aryan friends or
so-called friends—with servants, with the concierge, a former cook, a
business acquaintance—to be reclaimed upon our speedy return, as we all
hoped.

Some of us packed crates full of porcelain, glass, and silver, baskets full
of trousseaus of linen and clothing. Others were too paralyzed with terror
and fear to do more than sew money and gold into the lining of their
clothes. Some of them were successful. Everyone kept his method of hiding {his possessions} strictly secret. As for me, I packed the valuables precious to me—my color card file, some antiques—in a few boxes and left
them with my dear friends and clients, the Dr. Ms.,[3] who had enough
space for them in their country house and their small factory. I did not
want to burden them with clothing and linens. I sold a few pieces of
furniture and a few valuable pictures to some other friends.

I did not have any jewelry. My money was tied up in rental property
that, of course, I could not take along. A few other items—I forget what
they were—I took to my dear friend Mme Julie. Whoever found a way to
do it supplied himself with warm clothing for the imminent deportation:
ski suits, woolen things, heavy winter suits and fur or cloth winter coats,
and rucksacks. Brünn experienced a sales boom in rucksacks, as if war
were approaching. War was already upon us, only we did not know it yet.

The rucksack held everything we thought was necessary: a shoebrush, shoe polish, a toilet kit, underwear, extra shoes, house slippers, and that kind of stuff. We also took a little carryall for provisions and a canteen to be slung over the shoulder.

Then came the preparations for a variety of soft luggage consisting of a bed roll put together with featherbed, wool blanket, feather pillow, and sheets, which had to be tied on top of the rucksack or carried by hand, secured with carrying straps. I could tell by just looking at the poor depor tees, especially the old, ill, and feeble, or the ones too young and weak, how short a distance they would be able to carry such loads.

The roads and paths along which we were driven later on were strewn with the luggage left behind by the weakened, sweating, innocent victims of deportation. The Nazis and the populace (German and other nationalities alike) pounced like hyenas on the flotsam abandoned by their desperate, helpless fellow creatures. Only the younger, stronger "subhuman species" were capable of arriving at their goal, Theresienstadt, with their equipment and luggage nearly intact, only to see it "kanadized," "organized," that is, confiscated there and to see it disappear. More about that later. The only things remaining to them were the cash, the gold, and the jewelry.[4]

There were all kinds of hiding places, quite individualized. Everyone had his own secret hiding place. Many people hid these items in body cavities, only to have them discovered at the first body search and to be mistreated for hiding them.

Now I can reveal my hiding places, which were simple but effective. I rolled up rather large bank notes {in terms of size} and inserted them carefully into empty fountain pens and mechanical pencils. Bank notes of fairly larger denominations (1,000 to 2,000 Czech crowns) I rolled up and stored in empty cans of baby powder. I would open the cans, take out the powder, insert the roll of money, put the powder back, and seal them without a hint that they had been opened. Since powder had no value to anyone, it would remain in the rucksack, never stolen, never discovered.

Hiding places in the back of pictures or books, in shoe soles or heels, or in the lining of hats were useless, since they were well known and discovered immediately. Some places in the rucksack, {as well as} the carrying straps and handles, {could be used} if the rucksack and luggage had not been stolen or kanadized. As a whole we were well prepared for the big deportation. I only wish we had had no need for all these preparations.

2

EXPULSION, TRANSPORTS, AND ENTERING THE CAMP

After a lengthy pause I continue with my report. I keep pushing myself to continue the memoirs of this depressing period. In my mind I start over again and again, only to stop immediately. This hesitation, this postponement of the new beginning, is a {mental} block. I am incapable of collecting my thoughts, to order and arrange them so that the resumption {of my narrative} fits into a pattern with the previous record without appearing {to be} forced. I shall treat this chapter separately.

Before the arrival of the Nazis, Brünn had been home to a thriving Jewish community of 13,000 persons. A fraction of these, mostly young people, escaped abroad. The rest, approximately 10,000, were caught in the trap. Of these perhaps 6 percent returned alive. This statistic lies heavily on my heart. It includes many of my close relatives and dear friends who never returned. I must speak of them, since they were a part of my world. All these relatives who disappeared without a trace were not only old people whose clock of life was running down anyway. No, most of them were my contemporaries, or younger, at the peak of their healthiest and most productive years. Men, women, adolescents, and children, two generations were wiped out in that brief period.

The previous transport of people from Ostrau {Ostrava} to Nisko had already alerted us.[1] We feared that our turn would also come. We just did not know when lightning would strike. The mood was one of desperation, everyone racked his brains—where are they going to send us, and what shall I pack in my rucksack? How shall I prepare for the severe winter and the hot summer? Everyone tried to reduce his load to the absolute, indispensable minimum, and even that was too much, as we soon found out. We did not yet know at that time that even that minimum of possessions would be taken.

The dreaded day arrived when the pink slips were shoved under the doors of hundreds of victims, bearing the laconic notation: Summoned for February ——,1942 at 8:00 A.M. to the —— school on Merhaut Street for the purpose of deportation. This was a day of agony, terror, despair, tears, and the unbearable sensation that all of us were completely helpless; a feeling of injustice and deep fear.

Shortly afterwards I received a telephone call—my favorite sister, Alice, and her daughter, Dora, still a child, were in the transport;[2] a widow and an orphan without protection, left to fend for themselves. Alice was tearful but composed. I hurried to her apartment and helped her with her final packing. Then I accompanied her on the long way to the school, the assembly point. No one was allowed inside the school except the victims who were guarded by SS men. Saying farewell to those two was heart-breaking. Alice, among all my siblings, had been closest to me since child-hood: my playmate, protector, confidante, comforter, confessor; always ready to help me grow up. She was my haven when, as an adult, I myself went through some crises of the heart.

Alice and her husband, Artur, who unfortunately died of cancer at much too early an age, were my closest relatives and friends besides my mother, who had already died by that time. How could I forget her con-stant comfort and sympathy, her devoted affection to a brother who so frequently strayed and got involved in thoughtless affairs? How could I forget her caring and encouragement, and most of all her humor and wisdom? It was unbearable torture to have to accompany Alice and her little Dora, our Dora, to the impending deportation; to have to suppress tears, find words of comfort, when I myself was brokenhearted and in need of consolation. To part from the dearest of our friends, to see them disappear into the unknown, could only be compared to a farewell at the gates of the Underworld. Devastated, heartbroken, I finally reached my home after wandering around aimlessly.

From that time on transports of 1,000 each departed at regular intervals to the Ghetto Theresienstadt, the destination revealed to us by now. I could not have foreseen that I would meet Alice and Dora a few months later in Theresienstadt, only to be parted from them again after a few {months}, when both of them were sent once more on a transport, this time to "the East." Only a faint hope remained that we would ever meet again after the war. Who could have known that this was our final fare-well, that Fate would deprive me of the dearest, most faithful soul of all, Alice, who would disappear forever in the East? The majority of those in her transport were murdered by the assassins somewhere in the {woods} of Estonia.³ The younger, stronger slave laborers, Dora among them, survived. Dragged from camp to camp, near Reval {near Kohtla-Järve and Narva}, they were made to haul brick and other building materials. When the Russians advanced toward the West, the camps were transferred to the Reich. Dora had the incredible luck to be sent with a group from her camp near Hamburg to the neutral country of Sweden, after an enormous ransom had been paid for them. She now lives in Washington, D.C., and has taken her mother's place in my heart.

The subsequent transports decimated my family as well as my friends. My brother Ernst and his wife Stella and {two of their three living} children were summoned to the next transport. Their oldest son, Ludwig, had just been demobilized the previous year from the Pardubitzer Dragoons. He was a tall youngster, strong as a bear, and of a sunny disposition. At that time he was working as a forest laborer in a small village in Moravia, so that he could stay in touch with his girlfriend, a Czech schoolteacher, who taught in that village. Unfortunately, the girl had rejected a Czech suitor in favor of Ludwig.

Furiously, this man denounced Ludwig and the girl for rassenschande.⁴ As a consequence of this denunciation, Ludwig was immediately put into the next transport, thereby pulling his whole family after him. Fritz, his brother, a young medical student who had been forbidden to continue his studies and was working as a day laborer, was also summoned. The last two children were twins, Hans and Grete. Grete had died after a {short} illness at the age of sixteen, {several years} before the deportations began. Hans, a quiet, formal young man, was a talented cellist.

He attended every music festival in Czechoslovakia as well as abroad and had made friends with other cello aficionados. When Czechoslovakia's fate was sealed after Munich, English friends he had met in Trenčín {a town fifty miles southeast of Brünn in the Carpathian Mountains} invited him immediately to England. He was able to have his way against his

mother's objections and was thereby the only one of the family who escaped to a foreign country. During the war he lived in England, moved to
Canada in 1955, then ... to California where he {committed suicide}.

Again I was accompanying a part of my family to this accursed school
to bid them farewell. This time it was Ernst and Stella with Ludwig and
Fritz. I would see them later in Theresienstadt. My incomparable Sari, my
cook, housekeeper, devoted, faithful soul, had also been taken into that
transport.

She was still young, light-blond, slim, unsurpassed {as a cook}. She was
a Slovakian Jewess and could have easily returned to Slovakia and gone
into hiding there. Unfortunately, in spite of all warnings, she remained in
Brünn because of a German immigrant, a good-for-nothing, who exploited her, wormed money out of her, and I suspected that I was also
supporting him with my meager laborer's salary. They were summoned
together to the transport.

Soon there were only a few of my friends and relatives left in Brünn. I
still lived in the studio of Gustav Böhm, the painter.[5] I was lonely now
without my good and faithful Sari. It was a comfortable, almost luxurious
abode, with two attics in the front, a large studio looking out the back, a
malachite green tile stove, and Biedermeier furniture. No kitchen, but
hidden away in the adjacent attic an electric plate and washtub. With these
primitive tools—and without money—Sari had been able to conjure up
the most tasty meals.

Our optimistic belief that the day labor at Maloměřice would keep us
out of the transport proved to be illusory. One morning I found the pink
slip under my door. Even though we were aware of the transports, of
course, when it was one's turn, it was still a terrible shock. My stomach
was in knots; I was paralyzed with fear. I had to force myself to do something, anything, notwithstanding all the preparations I had already re-
hearsed. I had to pack, check my lists, making sure that I had not left

anything vital behind. I had to prepare an undetectable hiding place for the little money saved up for just this emergency, either somewhere on my body, or sewn into the luggage, as I described. To this day, after all these years, I still dream at times of packing the luggage, losing it, or having it stolen.

Every deportee was required to bring with him an inventory of the furnishings left behind as well as an inventory of all valuables, jewelry, money, stocks, real estate assets, etc., so that the Nazi gangsters would have no difficulty stealing the property of the Jewish subhuman rabble, and, of course, subhumans had no right to complain.

Early next morning I left my home that for so many years had granted me the illusion of a secure shelter and peace, the safe cave of a hunted animal. I had to lock the door and hand the key over to the Nazi blockwart {block warden}. Then I marched to the same school to which I had previously accompanied Alice, Ernst, and other friends. Loaded down with my rucksack, carryall, and tool kit, I reached my goal after a thirty-minute {walk}, sweating profusely.

The school looked new from the outside and was located near the textile school between Schwarzfeldgasse and Obrowitz {on Merhaut Street}. Heavily laden Jews from all parts of Brünn converged on this gate to the Underworld. In front of the school was a large lawn with a paved, elliptical driveway, like {one for} a theater; SS men everywhere, barking commands. I was exhausted, despondent, almost indifferent, resigned to my fate, but still berating myself—too late now—about having waited too long to escape and being caught in this trap.

After we, that is, I and the other 1,000 deportees, had entered the gate, we were sent to the gymnasium where we prisoners lined up in several long lines. Here, too, we were under the eye of SS guards to whom we had to hand all the completed forms, as required, and who yelled at us continually: "If we catch anyone hiding anything and he does not hand it over immediately—money, jewelry, or whatever—he will be shot." Many people in line were thus bullied into pulling their treasures out of their hiding places—a watch here, a brooch there, some other small item—and handing them over to the SS, only to see them disappear into the seemingly bottomless pockets of our tormentors.

This procedure took hours. Then we were told to go to the upper floor of the school and find some place to wait until next morning. Bent under the weight of our luggage, we stumbled up the stairs through a corridor to find a classroom where we could rest our tired limbs. There was a surprise waiting for us. There were no walls between any of the classrooms. All the doors from the corridor led into a single endless room in the new but ramshackle school. The ceiling beams were in place but the boards, some of which were not yet nailed down, were loosely laid next to each other over the floor joists. Vertical posts supported the ceiling beams everywhere.

The loose boards were covered with straw and excelsior as in a horse stable. This was our lodging. No food was provided. We had to feed ourselves from our rations in the carryalls. Water and primitive toilets were outside or in the cellar. We were told to be prepared to go on the transport that very night.

Everyone was too exhausted, mentally as well as physically, to even think of sleep. The shouting of the SS men, the bullying, the continuous {noise of} small children who screamed without understanding what was going on, {our} guarding the few belongings, losing them, finding them again. We looked at each other, horror-stricken. "You are here too, in the transport? I thought you had managed to escape abroad long ago." Smoking was forbidden because of the great danger of fire. Everyone tries in vain to gather his wits about him. When are we leaving? Where will they send us?

Around midnight the yelling of the SS, barked commands: "*Raus, raus,*

Waiting for transport.
(Courtesy Leo Baeck Institute)

line up by floors." We get up, line up, with rucksack, tool kit, carryall, canteen filled with water; screaming children pull their mothers this way and that; we move downstairs, line up in rows of four and move out of the gate. It is completely dark; the oval driveway is lined with torches stuck into the ground, SS men standing between the torches to make sure no one escapes. This picture is forever engraved in everyone's mind. This is sheer terror, the black uniforms of the SS, the closely ranked torches, the long somber rows of desperate human beings driven from their homes, destitute, defenseless, hopeless.

We try to resign ourselves to our fate, try to control our emotions. What crimes have we committed that we are being driven out of the town where we were born, where we grew up? We are too exhausted to think such disturbing thoughts. We pass through the gate and the long column assembles on the street fronting the school, guarded on both sides by SS men with torches; slowly we move forward in the direction of the Zeile {street in Brünn}.[6]

From time to time we notice figures standing, as if petrified, along the sidewalk; our esteemed fellow citizens, silent and cowed. On the Zeile long rows of trolley cars are awaiting our arrival. We board them, and they convey us through the blacked-out streets to our destination: the freight station behind the main railroad station. The tracks in the station glitter in the darkness from the light of the flashlights used by the SS men to direct the crowds to the waiting freight train that is ready to transport us far from our homes to a destination {revealed to us now}. Accompanied by SS shouts as well as kicks and shoves, we drag ourselves along a ramp through the darkness to the waiting cars. Old soldiers were only too well acquainted with these kinds of freight cars; they were called forty-and-eight; forty men or eight horses, so-called cattle cars; now they were stuffed full of human beings.

In the middle of the car, lengthwise, are one or two benches, only enough for seating half of the passengers. The rest stand, sit on the floor, or lean against the wall of the car. A bucket in the corner serves as latrine; near the ceiling a few air vents. The SS men count and recount, check the names on their lists. Then they bolt the sliding doors so they cannot be opened from the inside. Already we are imprisoned and defenseless. After a time, shouted orders, train whistles; then the train jerks a few times forward, back again, and then forward once more; the journey toward our . . . destination begins.

In spite of the air vents the freight car begins to be unbearably hot. People use the stinking buckets in front of everyone—an unaccustomed activity to which we become slowly accustomed. The stench is suffocating. After a while, however, one does not notice it anymore.

Totally exhausted, we begin to nod off. We lose all concept of time and place until dawn. Then we lift each other up to the air vents. The landscape of Bohemia and Moravia passes by outside, but we barely are able to perceive it. Without a window, looking merely through a slit, we can only see a small, {isolated} slice of the landscape {at a time}. From time to time the train stops; the SS men open a few of the sliding doors to air the freight cars. However, that only happens when there is a train coming from the opposite direction. At such times they let us get water for our canteens.

At one of the stations bread rations for every freight car are brought on. Everyone receives one-sixth of a loaf. They cram us back into the cars, lock the doors, and the train rolls on. We circle Prague by way of the freight stations and then continue in a northerly direction. We must have traveled sixteen to twenty hours. Night had fallen again, the train slowed down, stopped, a few more jerks, and we arrived.

Again the shouting: "Raus, raus, everybody out; take everything with you; line up by fours." We are in a little two-track railroad station with two sidings; a typical branch-line station: "Bohušovice-Bauschowitz," says the sign. We have reached our destination for the moment. We still did not yet know that for thousands it would be only a stop on the way to the East where all of them would die. For thousands of arrivals, especially the old people, it was the final destination.

Bauschowitz was the railroad station of the Fortress Theresienstadt. From the station a tree-lined road approximately two kilometers in length led to the gate of the fortress, which opened into the small town within the encircling ramparts and moats. Later on the inmates of the concentration camp, Fortress Theresienstadt, which was called "Ghetto Theresienstadt," built a single track with a separate siding from Bauschowitz into the center of the ghetto.

At last the doors of the freight cars {are} thrown open; fresh air replace{s} the unbearable body odor and the stench. Bleary-eyed figures, totally exhausted, deathly tired, unwashed, stumble . . . out of the cars: frightened women, children; the men, cursing their fate but still hoping. All of them grab . . . their rucksacks and their hand luggage and start . . . to move forward. The SS escort bark as usual and drive their 1,000 victims to {move at} a faster pace. The column {falls} into smaller groups. Despite all the yelling, the old people, weighed down by their luggage, simply {can} not continue and collapse . . . on the roadside. The frightened, starved children scream; the stronger people lumber forward under the weight of their luggage. The "Wandering Jew."

Ghetto Theresienstadt could not be seen at all from Bauschowitz. The only thing visible was an elongated green hill with a flat top and grass-covered slopes. The upper part of a church steeple rose abruptly out of the green belt, indicating that behind the green hill there had to be a town. The sloping hillsides were the fortification buildings of the Fortress Theresienstadt.

As the name implies, the fortress had been built in the time of the Empress Maria Theresa to secure the bridge over the Eger River {during

View of the church steeple.
(Courtesy Leo Baeck Institute)

the War of the Bavarian succession against Frederick II of Prussia}. The fortress had no intrinsic military value because it could easily be bypassed and the Eger could be crossed at other spots. Theresienstadt never heard or fired a shot in any serious situation. The road leading north from Prague passed by Theresienstadt and was also flanked by a fortification, the dreaded Little Fortress.[7] During the Austro-Hungarian monarchy, Theresienstadt had served as a garrison town, and it continued to be used as such during the existence of the Czechoslovakian Republic (1918–39).

The Little Fortress was the K.u.K. {imperial and royal} state prison where traitors and other political prisoners of the State rotted in their underground casemates {vaulted chambers}. The Serbian assassin who killed the Archduke Francis Ferdinand {Gavrilo Princip, 1893–1918}, thereby unwittingly precipitating World War I, was one of the prisoners of the fortress. After the end of the monarchy the murderer of the crown prince was set free and declared a national hero. All kinds of memorial plaques were dedicated to him. When Czechoslovakia became a protectorate of the Reich {March 25, 1939}, the plaques were removed only to be reinstated after the demise of the 1,000-year Reich. With such apparent ease history can be rewritten within a short period of time: 1914–45. It took only thirty years to turn a Serbian fanatic, misguided by nationalistic officers, from being a terrorist to a national hero, to a criminal subhuman, and back to a hero again.

I became all too well acquainted with Theresienstadt as well as the Little Fortress in the two and a half years I spent there. This time of my life is deeply engraved into my memory. The 300 sketches I had accumulated in Theresienstadt, and that I recovered miraculously after the war, were a great help to my memory, which after all had become just a bit rusty after thirty-five years in regard to names and details.

3

THERESIENSTADT

The road from Bauschowitz, as previously described, led through the fortress gate. First it crossed a kind of drawbridge over a deep moat. The grass-covered slopes stopped abruptly at brick walls, approximately fifteen to twenty meters in height. . . . [The walls, running in a zigzag line, had small, barred, white-painted gun embrasures.][1] Then came the moat[s], twenty to thirty meters wide, [{which were} dry and served for cultivating the vegetable and fruit orchards],[2] and on the other side of the moat[s] another brick wall of equal height with more embrasures, barred windows, and arched gateways—the entrances to the casemates that had originally housed the garrison personnel. These casemates could only be entered from inside the fortress. They consisted of brick-walled areas with walls one meter thick, topped with arched roofs that had been covered with dirt to a thickness of two to three meters and planted with grass.

Nearly all the casemates were used as housing for the inmates, as storerooms, and also as morgues. The gate on the exact opposite end of the town led again through walls and moats out of the fortress to a road across the Eger bridge, past the so-called sluice mill, and straight to the dreaded gate of the Little Fortress. Just before {the gate}, the road branched off toward Prague.

[Walls, moats, and fortifications formed a double ring around the town. As was customary during the baroque period, a fortification was laid out almost always with geometric precision in the usual star shape. The ramparts, moats, and fortifications had protruding and receding three- and five-cornered points, one side flanking the other.][3]

The fact that this town had only two entrances and was otherwise hermetically sealed off with ramparts and moats, thereby allowing for easy surveillance, was the precise reason that the SS hierarchy chose Theresienstadt as a ghetto. From a bird's-eye view Theresienstadt looked like an eight-pointed, elongated star. The sharp corners were formed by the entrenchments and the casemates; between them lay the deep moats now covered with gardens, meadows, and fields, then the grass-covered ramparts, following the same star design, and inside of this star nestled the typical fortress-cum-garrison town, with militarily aligned roadways, no nooks or crannies, square blocks of houses, five vertical streets, and [twelve cross streets {which} formed the simple street grid].[4]

The center consisted of a large square, customary for garrison towns since Roman times, for parades, public addresses, and meetings; two rather large parks; and two somewhat smaller parks. Plane trees {were} trimmed to a rectangular shape. [When these trees were not covered with thick foliage, their cropped, unnatural limbs displayed grotesque shapes that could have easily caused ghostly nightmares in anyone with a lively imagination. In the middle of the trees was the sandy parade ground surrounded by a street and sidewalks.

Along the sidewalks, symmetrically aligned, the abandoned church and parsonage. Around the corner the two schools (now children's homes), across from it the gendarmerie barracks, now ghetto housing, adjacent to the headquarters townhouses and businesses. On the fourth side again large houses with businesses that had been evacuated; the corner was occupied by the former city hall (rathaus) built in an overly ornate style, {with} mansard roof {a roof with two slopes on each of four sides, the lower steeper than the upper} and corner tower. That building became the dreaded and feared SS headquarters, or kommandatur, the administrative building.][5] All orders issued from that building. [The offices of the SS headquarters occupied all three floors of the former city hall.

In the cellar (basement) of the city hall were the cells of the military court with which I involuntarily became very well acquainted at a later date. The headquarters stood on a corner formed by the square and one of the vertical streets. The corner itself was taken up by a four-story tower with the black SS flag waving from its top. The SS troops lived in the special kameradschaftsheim {living quarters}, the only small, modern hotel that had belonged to the earlier garrison.][6] [{It served} as housing, dining room, and tavern for the SS.][7] The Czech gendarmes, still in their old uniforms but with the Nazi emblem on their caps, were employed as guards, and they were housed at a distance from these living quarters.

The SS garrison was completely separated from the ghetto population by a high wooden fence that crisscrossed the streets and the edges of the square. These fences provided the SS with a Judenrein {"Jew-free," a Nazi term} corridor. [{They were} surrounded by barbed wire so that the SS would never have to mingle with the Jews crossing the square. This exclusivity was carried to the point that from the barbed wire fence, a barbed wire–fenced walkway led from the headquarters to the living quarters, five blocks away. That part was totally off limits to the Jews and forced them of course to make additional detours.]8 Several roomy casemates located beneath the entrenchments also went under the name of barracks. One of these {the Kavalier barracks} served as a sort of improvised insane asylum. The Nazis had cleared all Reich insane asylums of Jewish patients and had sent the poor wretches on the transport to Theresienstadt.

[An unnamed barracks served as mortuary, where the coffins were piled four and five high. The deceased of the previous day would be put into the coffins the next morning (the coffins were manufactured in the lumberyard) and put on a flat cart, and since we had no horses or trucks, these carts were pushed and pulled by manpower. The coffins were deposited in the mortuary in the casemate from where they would be transported for burial. In 1941–42 the coffins were buried in regular graves in an improvised cemetery.]9 [Dispersed throughout the grid, now considerably reduced, {were} the gigantic barracks, typically utilitarian: a gate, evenly spaced windows, mostly barred, always amazingly large courtyards, vaulted galleries with arched arcade openings. Doors led from the open galleries into the different living quarters.]10 The barracks were given the names of German cities to replace the original Czech names: Hamburger, Dresdner, Hannover barracks, etc.

The Magdeburger barracks was the center, a kind of office building, the nerve center of the administration, and since the inmates had been made to believe that they possessed a sort of autonomy, it was the office for the various secretariats of the administration {or government} called the Ältestenrat (Council of Elders), such as the department of maintenance, sup-

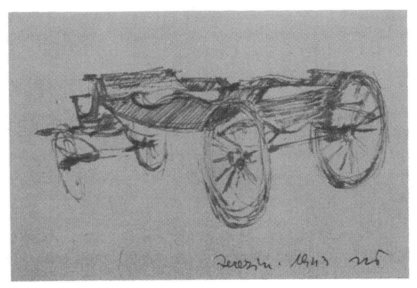

Death cart.
(Courtesy Leo Baeck Institute)

plies, health care, transports, justice, propaganda [by order of the Gestapo], statistics, etc.

The seven members of the Council of Elders also lived in the Magdeburger barracks, together with hundreds of the privileged inhabitants from the AK1 and AK2, of whom I shall speak later.[11] The Dresdner and Hamburger barracks were exclusively reserved for women and children; the Hannover for men. The Sudeten barracks, formerly the armory and equipment depot, was assigned to men only where they were housed in gigantic dormitories with a total capacity of 6,000 people. [The Hohenelbe barracks became the main hospital and contained an operating room.][12] {It was} the former garrison hospital, an old-fashioned but solidly built and airy hospital, with a well-equipped operating room. Attached to it were, I believe, five ancillary sickrooms (sort of emergency wards), small hospitals for approximately 100 patients without surgery rooms. In addition, there were four sickrooms that were set up in the private houses in four different districts.

[The former Theresienstadt elementary and secondary school was the children's home, which was very well run by professional educators. Our adminstration took great pains to keep as many young people as possible out of the transports, and to save them, if at all possible, for the longed-for peace. The Nazis shattered this hope. Only a few {700} of the 7,000 or more children survived the war.][13]

A well-furnished bakery was taken over and was put into operation, as well as a small power plant and waterworks. The kitchen installations proved to be too small, as they were planned to feed only 3,500 soldiers. The population rose to a maximum of 50,000 persons within a short time and remained on the average around 40,000.[14] New, primitive but well-organized kitchen installations were ingeniously improvised in the individual houses.

The so-called Jewish "self-government" received their curt orders every morning, when a small delegation of the Council of Elders had to appear at the SS headquarters, and these orders had to be executed without any objection or contradiction. They were immediately handed on, in transcript or so-called file entries, to the lower echelons of the administration.

What I have described here was the development over a period of months. When Theresienstadt was declared a ghetto, it was merely a small garrison town without a garrison and with a population of about 3,500 Catholic souls and cleared of any Jews. Reluctantly, these people had to evacuate their town, their houses, their businesses, brothels, churches, hospital, post office, offices, schools, etc., to make room for the new inhabitants. . . . The remainder of the town consisted of two-story houses for the civilian population. . . . {After Theresienstadt} was turned into a ghetto, the civilian population was evacuated {in June 1942}. . . . [They did, however, have the advantage of unlimited possibilities to resettle anywhere in the country with friends or relatives, with compensation. A formerly living organism became a dead town to be taken over by the Jews. The town was not altogether dead, [however]. The departing population had left an army of bedbugs, fleas, and lice behind.][15]

{Earlier} the Jewish Community of Prague, on orders from the Gestapo, summoned first 1,500 and then another 1,500 "volunteers," strong, ablebodied young men of different professions and skills, who then were sent to Theresienstadt, there to organize, in the role of pioneers, a ghetto with the intention of increasing the population of that town tenfold. These volunteers were given a note and an insignia: "AK1" and "AK2," *aufbaukommando* (construction detail). The 3,000 young men {actually 1,342} enjoyed privileges and had a special status, granted them by the Gestapo. The town was {still inhabited by its gentile residents} when the first privileged transports, AK1 and AK2, . . . arrived from Prague.[16]

The Council of Elders recruited their leading department heads out of their ranks, as well as production managers, chief physicians, managers of the power plants, gas as well as electricity, and the waterworks.

The most important privilege consisted in the fact that the newcomers had been assured exemption from all transports. That exemption included five persons from {each of} their immediate families, which meant that AK1 and AK2 with their families, numbering 15,000 altogether, were exempt from all further transports.[17]

[A short time later the first transports from Brünn and smaller cities rolled into the ghetto. Terrible chaos occurred that was resolved, however, within a short time. Thousands of Jews were arriving continually who had to be housed and nourished and put again into the cursed trains to be transported East.][18]

Having only just arrived, we, of course, were not aware of these facts. At that time {people from} newly arrived transports were completely unaware of the existence of "transports to the East," of the horrible truth that Theresienstadt was nothing more than a transit station to the extermination camps of the East. After our arrival in Theresienstadt, we soon learned of these facts.

A few days after my arrival I was so happy to see Alice and Dora, my faithful Sari, and many of my friends from Brünn, to be united with them again, only to see them, helpless and broken in spirit, become a number in a new transport. This farewell was irrevocable and forever. The scourge of the continual transports lasted until the end of the war. When I arrived with my transport in Theresienstadt in March of 1942,[19] a crowd of previous arrivals awaited us, searching for familiar faces of friends and relatives. A few members of the Council of Elders were also present. Like all those {from the} transports we too spent the first two nights in the Jaeger barracks quarantine. Then men and women were separated.

The women and children lived in crowded quarters in the Hamburger and Dresdner barracks. We men were stuffed into the Sudeten barracks, in storerooms with two to three level plank beds, hurriedly nailed together and covered with excelsior-filled mattresses. . . . Shortly after our arrival in the Theresienstadt Ghetto, still in the Jaeger barracks with its excelsior-covered stone floors, where we were totally exhausted, numb, perplexed, and filled with anxiety about the transports to the East, several of the gentlemen from the Council of Elders, as well as previously arrived ghetto residents, came to see us, armed with the list of members of our transport. That is how Alice, Dora, Ernst, Ludwig, and Sari found me. Later on other young men, functionaries of different administrative departments, came in search of specialists.

Two of them, as I found out later, were not merely heads of departments, but members of the Council of Elders, the "government." One of them, Ing. {Engineer} Zucker, I knew from the Jewish community in

Brünn; the other was Ing. Gruenberger, head of the technical department of the ghetto.[20] To my great surprise they had heard of my reputation as a competent architect. I was greatly relieved and reassured when they informed me that I would be hired for the technical department as an architect after I had served my required weeks of forced labor. They would make sure that I would not be put into a transport to the East.

The two of them and my immediate superior, Erich Kohn,[21] were, so to speak, my guardian angels until the time when I and they as well, unfortunately, were transported to the East. With their help I could also be my sister Ida's guardian angel to a limited extent.

Every male arrival had to do the usual day laborer's work without pay {in return} for bed and bad food before he could be drafted into the work force of the ghetto. Every able-bodied man without exception had to serve as grave digger {until he was given another function in the ghetto}, a profession singularly foreign to most of us. Those men, however, who had been drafted to active work service by the Nazis before the ghetto {had been established}, where they had learned to dig trenches, foxholes, and camouflage positions, knew the work well. There is not much difference between digging trenches and graves {graeben und graeber}.

A cemetery had been installed on a section of the entrenchment, first in a hodgepodge manner, without any visible order, later in regular rows. Everything was in shades of dull brown, with little wooden slats as headstones, indicating the name, place of origin, and date of death of the deceased. In time the dates were washed away by rain and snow. The cemetery work went on for a long time. The old people, hopeless and undernourished, susceptible to all kinds of diseases, died like flies.[22]

Wrapped in a sheet, they were buried in a simple coffin nailed together from six rough boards. The attending family members would repeat the rabbi's prayers dry-eyed. Death was a daily occurrence. In spite of the

Cemetery.
(Courtesy Leo Baeck Institute)

grief, the immediate family members, if there were any, would breathe a sigh of relief. They were rid of the worry of seeing their dear old ones sent to the East to their death and knew they had been spared unbearable suffering.

[Later—1942—a modern crematorium was built close by, in front of the ramparts, to save the expense of the coffins. The ashes of the deceased were poured into a cardboard box on which the pertinent dates were registered. Due to the presence of so many old people and the large mortality figures, the boxes piled up and casemates were used to range them along the walls, row after row; in time they were piled ten high.][23]

Shortly before {the end of the war}, {the SS} had destroyed everything that could bear witness to their misdeeds. Hundreds of thousands of boxes filled with ashes of the cremated Jewish inmates of Theresienstadt were poured into the Eger River.[24] Just visualize how many thousands of Sudeten Germans, fanatical Nazis, must have drunk the water of the Eger that flowed into the Elbe River, water permeated with the ashes of dead Jews. Serves them right!

During the "Twilight of the Gods," {(the end of the Reich as in Wagner's opera of that title) the Nazis} also unfortunately managed to destroy all irreplaceable documents and archives of the murderous extermination activity of the SS throughout Europe.[25] These archives had been stored in the huge vaults of the Sudeten barracks.

After my arrival, having worked the prescribed three weeks as grave digger, I was transferred from labor conscription by Ing. Gruenberger and Zucker, who, as I mentioned before, had heard of me and had interviewed me upon my arrival. The next day I began my job with the technical department. In a large vaulted room—I believe it was the Magdeburger barracks, the office building, the center of the ghetto administration—stood rows of drafting tables, manned by younger and older architects who stood or sat in front of them and drew. I knew none of them, but within a short time we were well acquainted, no jealousies, no pecking order except for the department head. My new colleagues came from different parts of the country and different training. Some were arrogant—those with prominent reputations—they were the butt of biting jokes and criticism. They had no choice; they had to adapt and to get in line with the rest of us. There were a few antisocial elements who were unbearable and troublemakers in spite of their expertise. These people, who behaved like neurotic, inbred schnauzers, made it very difficult for the rest of us to maintain even a semblance of harmony with the constraints of working and living in close quarters.

[It did not take us long to find out that Theresienstadt was a contaminated, vile place. It is a miracle that no epidemics erupted. The people must have been immune.[26] Dozens of the wells in the houses were contaminated. Cesspool water seeped through the earth into the wells. . . .

Wherever we went, we found the housing full of vermin, bedbugs, lice, and millions of fleas. Coming back from such surveys, our calves were bitten and full of fleas that we could only remove with kerosene. It was much harder not to bring the bedbugs and fleas into our housing.][27]

Our office manager . . . Erich (Era) Kohn . . . was young, I believe twenty-six, twenty-seven, a Czech architect, a Communist. In spite of his youth he was accepted by everyone as head of the office, respected as thoroughly competent, and esteemed for having won several {architectural} competitions. He also was undoubtedly an original thinker, highly gifted, almost a genius. He was more than merely talented; he had fully absorbed modern and historical literature, and he was good-looking to boot. He belonged, of course, to the AK1 group, and his position was influential because he was closely acquainted with the Council of Elders and with most of the AK1 and AK2, who held the most important positions in the ghetto and enjoyed their confidence and their respect. He would critique us severely, even ruthlessly, therefore everyone tried to do his very best.

In spite of all his good traits Era was extremely neurotic and had a tendency to experience uncontrollable bouts of towering rage. These attacks were almost ludicrous, because at the height of such an attack he would flee to his desk and hide his head in the desk's top drawer. Genius must be forgiven certain foibles.

We, his colleagues, always forgave him everything though we were annoyed by his fits. Aside from respecting his extraordinary talent, we really liked him for all his other humane qualities. As young as he was, he exhibited an almost fatherly loyalty toward his fellow workers. Whether he liked or disliked one or the other was immaterial. He stood up for all of them. In our department we were assured of his protection and, thereby, of protection that at that time represented the difference between life and death. This protection asserted itself anytime the transports to the East were assembled.

4

"PROTECTION"

Before continuing with the report of my life and the fate of my relatives, I want to discuss the matter of the transports to the East and the importance of "protection" connected with them. Even today this chapter in the history of Theresienstadt troubles and depresses every one of the victims, witnesses, participants, whatever we might call ourselves. Self-doubts arise in all of us, doubts about our ethics, our humanity, fairness, justice, and decency. It was the time when we were forced by unforeseen, desperate, critical, life-threatening circumstances to relinquish hesitantly, slowly, unhappily, all rules, laws, and principles of decency, etc. We had to rationalize our own behavior to the point where we accepted the fact of our own demoralization and corruption. Who can say today whether all of this was inexcusable? The facts mentioned herein forced the people affected by these difficult times to act in ways that others would only do reluctantly. It must be clear that such actions were defensible because an inescapable fate forced their hand. There is simply not that much justice in our world.

I had previously reported about my arrival in Theresienstadt and my integration into the work force. The concept of "protection," at times secured through {one's position} in the work force, was of such paramount importance for all of us that it overshadowed any other considerations. After our arrival in the ghetto it took only a few hours of {discussion} with previous arrivals to make us comprehend that the ghetto was by no means a permanent place of residence. Gripped with unspeakable fear we watched the transports to the East depart almost every week.[1] It was easy to figure out when one's number would be up if one had to watch helplessly as relatives and friends were assigned to the transports going east and one was powerless to prevent it.

This is what happened to me during the second week of my Theresienstadt stay, when I had to watch my sister, Alice, her daughter, Dora, and Sari, my housekeeper, being put into the transport. They disappeared and I was incapable of preventing it.[2] Only a few months later I could have extended my "protection" to them. Thus I quickly realized the tragic vulnerability of our situation. I had to readjust in order to survive. I witnessed the dumb despair of those condemned to go on the transport when they were crammed into the cattle cars. The cattle car became the ferry of Charon, the ferryman on the River Styx leading to the Underworld; forty people or eight horses.

Everyday life continued unabated as if it were a small town of 7,000 inhabitants now suddenly grown to 40–50,000. There was work and leisure, concerns with sanitation, housing, health care, child care, record keeping, construction, theater, concerts, lectures, all functioning as well as possible under the circumstances. Life pulsated with incredible optimism, fatalism, with life-affirming self-deception, with never-ending hope so inherent in the Jewish people. It seemed at times almost normal, carefree, without much thought. A roof, some soup, and one-eighth of a loaf of bread were provided. Surviving was everything. These short, carefree periods of continually disappointed hope were disrupted periodically by the inhuman eastern transports.

At such time, a living organism of 30–40,000 people would suffer a collective, partially paralyzing stroke. Someone saw Eichmann or Möhs[3] go into the Magdeburger central office. Immediate, all-pervading paralysis. Whose turn would it be? Perhaps mine? Who of my family is on the list? One saw gripping fear in everyone's eyes—with the exception of the "protected," of course. The Council of Elders had to bear the burden of having to make the selection for the transport assignment during their nightlong conference.

Transports numbered usually 1,000 or 2,000. There were transports for elders, the helpless sick elders torn from their children, transports of fifty- to seventy-year-olds, so sad, cruel, deadly. It was a continual, desperate struggle to avoid being assigned to a transport, not to be transported to death somewhere in the East. In fear of death one forgets, slowly at first, but then with considerable speed, the rules of ethics, of decency, of helpfulness, as well as all the other rules that were part and parcel of our upbringing, imprinted on us from infancy, at home and at school; rules that up until now we had lived by. I want to live. I do not want to see either my mother or my sisters, my brother, my children, nieces, and nephews go to their death; the instinct of self-preservation. What happened to ethics? At any and all costs we try to prevent the execution of the death sentence on us and our loved ones.

Whoever has not lived for a few weeks, months, or even years in such a situation can hardly comprehend the indescribably immense power, the insuperable force of self-preservation. An armed soldier can defend himself, fight for his life. We, the helpless, unarmed prisoners, outcasts, deprived of any support from the population at large, were a defenseless subspecies of humanity at the mercy of our fanatical, mortal enemies, the SS Supermen.

The ghetto seemed to us like paradise at the time; a kind of security blanket to which we clung, surrounded by others of our kind with the same fate, the same worries. We felt that leaving it would mean certain death; later on this feeling became a certainty. To escape that fate one had to do everything to be included in the privileged group of the "protected." The battle for protection was all-inclusive and everyone sought to gain entry into the privileged group, or to find a "protected" protector who would hide him under his wings. Thus began my road to "protection," a successful road until two and a half years later, when I lost this protection through other circumstances that I will explain later. At the last, toward the end of the war, even my most influential protectors lost their own "protection." The entire Council of Elders with the exception of Murmelstein was murdered.[4] And so I have arrived at my point of departure a few pages back: the technical department and our boss, Era Kohn.

At the time when the Brünn Jews were deported to Theresienstadt in the winter of 1941–42, the organization of the ghetto was still in its beginning stages. The cemetery did not yet contain more than about 100 graves. The many Jews driven out of their home districts within the republic quickly took over and filled the small town of Theresienstadt, surrounded with fortifications without the possibility of expanding the existing space. . . . The little town had to organize or rather improvise hurriedly to accommodate a tenfold and larger population and provide housing, a centralized food supply, kitchens, toilets, washrooms, hospitals, lights, a sewage system, and dozens of other necessities for an organized community that had to be built from scratch. Thus arose in miniature . . . an organized state with a central administration and all the necessary institutions, subdivisions, departments, bureaucracies, ministries of a miniature republic with extremely limited authority, controlled by the SS. They had to accept unquestioningly the daily orders from the SS headquarters.

{The} transport of 1,500 young volunteers, selected by the Prague Jewish Community, {that} arrived in Theresienstadt counted among them{selves} a number of experts, engineers, architects, doctors, artists, and other professionals, but also the vocational professions of cook, baker, carpenter, farmer, gardener, tailor, and cobbler were represented among them. Their leaders were the diplomatic Jakob Edelstein, a very brilliant, youngish, Zionist youth leader; Ing. Zucker and Ing. Gruenberger, both civil engineers; the previously mentioned, talented young architect, Era Kohn; and others. They represented the core of Theresienstadt, the establishment, the administration via Berlin. The Gestapo in Prague that had developed the idea of the Ghetto Theresienstadt had promised these Prague Jews of the construction commandos certain privileges. They pretended to have planned Theresienstadt as a model for many other Jewish ghettos in the other occupied countries. This was, of course, one of the uncounted examples of "the treachery of the Nibelungen," tricks, deceit, lies, perfidies. Theresienstadt became the transit camp of the Czech, Moravian, Austrian, and German Jews on their way to extermination in the East.

The privileges of the AK commandos were manifold. {Membership on} the Council of Elders, all the key positions in all departments, subdivisions, public service, all food and water distribution, waterworks, gasworks, agriculture, hospital kitchens, and sewage system were held by AK1 and AK2 members.

As the population increased, however, even newcomers like myself were given public service positions. The members of the council had the privilege of separate housing in the administration barracks, the Magdeburger barracks. The other administrative employees found quarters for themselves, sometimes in groups, sometimes single quarters. Cooks, bakers, and doctors had no trouble finding group housing at their places of work. To own separate accommodations was the dream of every inmate who fancied himself to be one of the "permanent" ones. Such quarters were called kumbals.

Cook, baker, food distributor, and warehousing manager were the most privileged, sought-after jobs. They provided enough food to eat one's fill and to have some left over for illegal barter for cigarettes. Smoking was strictly forbidden, but everyone smoked. Anyone who smoked shared his cigarette by individual puffs among his family or friends. The possession of money was also forbidden, but most people had some money, nevertheless. If you were caught with money or cigarettes during one of the many raids, it meant criminal proceedings, assignment to the next transport East, and certain death. In spite of that, large amounts of cigarettes continued to appear in the ghetto. Not the Czech crown {currency} but the cigarettes served as the small change of the ghetto.

The price of cigarettes was pushed up by the raids, by the ban, and, of course, by the threat of transport in case {one was} caught. Ten cigarettes equaled one-half to one loaf of bread. For someone who was not a baker, a loaf of bread was priceless. Everyone starved except the cooks and the bakers. Hunger boosted the price of the daily bread and therefore the price of the cigarettes. Money existed but was a scarce item.

The Gestapo, the SS, and the gendarmes, on the other hand, were eager to obtain our cash. And so a complicated chain of black-marketing developed, condoned by and a profitable financial arrangement for the SS and others involved. Among the camp inmates there were only a few known black marketeers who worked hand in hand with the Czech gendarmes during their weekly tour of duty. With the knowledge and participation of the SS, the gendarmes brought whole suitcases and rucksacks full of cigarettes into the ghetto without any control. These cigarettes disappeared nightly into the hiding places of the middleman black marketeers and from there through a chain of other minor black marketeers, unobtrusively they would find their way to the smokers and bread barterers. There was a 500–1,000 percent profit for gendarmes and SS. There would be many raids and transport sentences to support the price level of the cigarettes. The SS was always ready whenever and wherever there was something to acquire or to steal.

Here I somewhat digressed from discussing the privileges of the AK1 and AK2. Their most important privilege was the solemnly promised permanent protection against transports. This privilege protected every member of the AK commandos including the immediate family, parents, wife, and children, up to five persons, from eastbound transports. Thus $3,000 \times 5 = 15,000$ camp inmates were protected against the fate that threatened from the East.[5] This fact was the motivation for our increasingly cynical, corrupt attitude of "each man for himself." When I saw my sister Alice and Dora disappear on their way to hell—on an eastern transport— helpless to save them, I determined to find "protection" at any price. (I realized later that Ing. Zucker and Ing. Gruenberger held a protective hand over me.) I watched young women pursue single AK1 and AK2 men desperately for their protection through a ghetto marriage {a marriage valid in the ghetto}. It wasn't easy for the young men to make the right choice out of the crowd {of girls}. The rest of us had to search feverishly for other means of transport "protection."

Here I want to explain briefly how I found the necessary protection for myself and, later, also for my sister Ida Bunzl-Federn from Prague. As a newcomer, I had to discover first who had the authority to grant protection and who had the almost divine power of selection, of making the decisions between life and death, assigning persons into as well as excluding them from the transports.

In the beginning, I assumed rather naively that the SS issued the orders and made the selection as they had done in Brünn when they sent us to Theresienstadt. That was not the case here. With devilish baseness and cunning they did dictate the number of victims to be sent east, but they put the burden of selection on the Jews themselves; to select their own coreligionists, relatives, their friends. In the end this unbearable, desperate, cynical burden destroyed the community leaders who were forced to make the selections. The power over life and death forced on the Council of Elders was the main reason, the unavoidable force, behind the ever-increasing corruption in the ghetto; its single, solitary goal was life and "protection" from transports.

Within a short time I grasped the method and procedure of the transport selections. Normally there were merely three days between the order given and the departure of the transport. Within this time span all activity in the ghetto halted as if [it were] paralyzed. Everyone's concentration focused on one fact only: whether they or their family members were "in it."

When the notice with the fatal assignment arrived, they would mobilize all their powers of influence and connections to smuggle a letter to a member of the selection committee of the Council of Elders, who met throughout the night, begging them desperately to remove them or a mother, sister, or child from the list. Single individuals had little chance to escape transports. Fearing further transports, I asked my colleagues in the department what to do and they advised me to talk to Era Kohn. When I voiced my fears to him he said brusquely: "You are on my 'protection' list, like everyone else here. Besides that you are also on the list of my bosses,

Ing. Zucker and Gruenberger." What a surprise. That took a load off my mind and from that time on I was "protected."

At every transport Era Kohn fought successfully for his architects. (I survived twenty-eight transports.) His influence within the Council of Elders was considerable, and our work was indispensable for the development of the ghetto. Era Kohn truly deserves the space given to him in this narrative. After the liberation, I heard that he had survived and was working in Prague as an architect. He was a good man, talented, intelligent, always willing to help and stick up for a friend.

Of course, every department head had his list of indispensable employees whom he wished to protect. Over time my position as one of the architects in the engineering department increased in importance and in security. For example, I had received a commission to draw a large bird's-eye view of Theresienstadt and the surrounding area. This commission included a permit allowing me to leave the ghetto daily and to roam freely within a radius of three kilometers (who was going to measure the exact distance covered?) so I could make preliminary sketches. Another commission consisted of designing two rooms for a Potemkin {false front} "museum" to exhibit all the accumulated statistical graphs that were routinely produced by the group of artists headed by Fritta[6] as well as my big bird's-eye perspective, just in case the Red Cross Commission might ever show up. Other assignments included the rather risky order to design a dining room and bar in the kameradschaftsheim of the SS, at their hotel, as well as other less desirable work such as planning the latrines and barracks and preparing working drawings for the bauhof {lumberyard}, the cabinetmaker shops of the ghetto.

After having consolidated my protected position in our department by becoming indispensable, I looked for ways and means to increase it {the sphere of protection} and make it even more secure, so it would include my sister and her husband and two daughters, newly arrived from Prague. Era, my boss, assured me that he could put one more person on his "protection" list and advised me to find some connections directly within the decision-making body of the Council of Elders. By an incredible stroke of luck I managed to make such connections.

Ing. Zucker, an influential member of the Council of Elders, lived with his beautiful and cultivated young wife in the Magdeburger barracks. She worked in the farming section {the gardens outside the wall}. They had a room with two primitive wooden bunks, a table, two stools nailed together from boards; not a very attractive abode. One day he called me to his office and said that one time in Brünn he had seen apartments I had decorated. He wanted to know if I could design for him a halfway livable, practical, yet still-attractive interior {that would give him} privacy with the materials available in the ghetto, such as boards, sheets, and blankets. I readily accepted the commission, especially as I already had some experience in "furnishing" minimal lodgings, anywhere from four to twelve square meters under staircases and in attics for several bakers, cooks, and gardeners. . . . This commission represented the "connection" that I had so urgently sought. A member of the Council of Elders could legally request boards, sheets, and nails from the lumberyard and from other warehouses inaccessible to the rest of us. We "organized," that is, we stole, wherever we could, at night and at great risk. Council of Elders members were also entitled to the use of hot plates, an indispensable {item}. To this day it remains a mystery to me how all the hot plates, being strictly forbidden, found their way into the ghetto; probably the same way the cigarettes did {since} using a hot plate . . . was a punishable offense.

The small power plant of the fortress, designed for 7,000–8,000 inhabitants, was ill-suited for 40,000–50,000. Almost every afternoon between 5:00 and 7:00 there would be electrical short circuits and raids {in re-

Zucker's kumbal.
(Courtesy Leo Baeck Institute)

sponse}. When the lightbulbs would begin to flicker you knew people were cooking. To avoid the continual raids by authorities we instituted a kind of self-discipline, watched over by the room leaders, and thereby we reduced the power use and extended the periods of available electricity. The techniques used to hide the hot plates, to camouflage them, to connect illicit electric lines to the few {existing} outlets, became an art form.

I trust the reader will forgive my digression from my intended topic—finding connections for "protection." After I decorated Ing. Zucker's habitation to his great satisfaction, Ing. Gruenberger asked me to furnish his lodgings {as well}. He also had a young wife, and the Council of Elders members were entitled to share their housing with their wives. {As I have already noted}, all other ghetto residents were strictly separated by gender: men in the Sudeten barracks, women in the Hamburger and Dresdner barracks. Only the barracks commandants and later on the privileged owners of kumbals were exempt from that general rule.

I am afraid I digress time and again from the subject of transport "protection." {Faced day and night with} hunger and galloping corruption, under the incessant, demoralizing fear of death, I do not believe there are many people who have the dignity, courage, the fearlessness to face death bravely without any weapon, without any means of resistance. Most of us were young, without any resources or weapons to resist the menacing death. Our heroism consisted in waiting without hope for the inevitable end; to accept it without lamentation or despair. But human beings cling to life, and fighting against death seems to be a law of nature, to do anything and everything for as long as possible to assure oneself of another sunrise.

History teaches us that man never was very choosy when it came to methods {and} means {to try} to stay alive. Who could blame us, condemned to ghettos and other concentration camps, if ethical maxims were slowly displaced by the instinct for self-preservation, and {we} all became corrupted in the desperate flight toward "protection"? Our ship is sinking; it is each man for himself. Let the others drown, jump into the lifeboat, try to reach land.

The psychological corruption affecting all of us, including me, presented in my view the most difficult problem after the war; we all had to deal with it, to overcome it, before we could regain our mental balance. How can I forgive myself for having succumbed to egotistical, ruthless, incomprehensible actions toward my fellow sufferers whenever danger threatened; for being concerned solely with "protection" for my defenseless sister Ida and myself? I have tried {in vain} to drive this depressing, disquieting problem into my subconscious, to bury it there, if possible. Bringing this chapter of my memoirs out of the depths is therefore truly a difficult task for me.

The chapter does not merely speak of my life under most trying circumstances in the ghetto and the subsequent concentration camps, but it forces me to exhume the almost forgotten ghosts of the past and their nameless graves.

5

THE TRANSPORTS

I will now try to recreate the atmosphere, the conditions, prevailing during a transport to the East, only one of the {twenty-eight} that I survived before it was my turn to be put on one of them, after I was imprisoned in the Little Fortress. I choose to describe this scourge of our Theresienstadt ghetto existence right here at the beginning, because every other aspect of our ghetto life paled in comparison to it.

After four to six weeks of routine activity in the ghetto, we began to regain our equilibrium. Everyone works at the assigned job, the men visit the women and children in the women's barracks. Young men and women stroll or sit on the few available benches or in the parched grass in the park or on the grass-covered roof of the Jaeger barracks, our main recreational park. Three times a day we get in line at one of the seven kitchens in town to fetch the food. The opera group rehearses in an attic, accompanied and coached by Maestro Schächter,[1] a man obsessed with music, on the one and only sickly sounding piano in the ghetto. A trio performs in the evening in the courtyard of the Dresdner barracks. Rabbi Leo Baeck[2] is giving one of his wise and brilliant lectures; we play cards, we try to forget where we are.

Someone in the so-called Gendarmerie barracks, that belongs to the ghetto housing complex, watches from his window as a car stops in front of the SS headquarters directly opposite. Two SS men whom we do not know (later on we know them too well; we call them the "birds of death") alight from the cars. They turn out to be Eichmann from Berlin and Möhs from Prague. The man at the window turns white, becomes very still; his stomach tightens. He calls his comrades to the window; one look is enough. One word slowly forms on his lips: "transport." Within minutes the barracks echoes with the damned, cursed word: transport. Within five minutes 4,000 inmates are aware of the transport being assembled.

No one sleeps that night. Next morning all activities cease. Fear, deepest pessimism, silent sorrow fill everyone. Who can work under such pressure? Will it be me and my family? As it is their daily custom, the Council of Elders go to report to {SS} headquarters and to receive their orders. They return at 11:00 A.M. with ashen faces. A transport of 1,000 Jews has to be assembled immediately; within two days they must be ready to be loaded into the train that is waiting at Bauschowitz, the nearest railroad station.

The Council of Elders retire immediately to the conference room and take the complete list of names {of inmates} in the ghetto with them.

Hohenelbe park.
(Courtesy Leo Baeck Institute)

Before long the various department heads appear with their lists of "indispensables" who are absolutely necessary for the running of the ghetto. The fight for the "protected" erupts. Out of 45,000 inmates, 27,000 were protected or ineligible for deportation: the Council of Elders, AK1 and AK2 and their families: 15,000; the indispensable staff from all departments: 3,000 to 5,000; 800 to 1,000 inmates too severely ill to be transported; 2,000 small children and their mothers; and 4,000 seniors over seventy.

No one envies the Council of Elders their power over life and death. We know that they spend sleepless nights, burdened by the responsibility to make impartial selections. The 1,000 persons to be selected from the 10,000–15,000 are not just numbers as we all know, not faceless masses. At stake are our brothers, our essence, all of us. The unbearable burden of transport selections imposed on the Council of Elders by the SS, of sending their own brothers to certain death in the East, became too much for most of them in spite of the constant repetition of the process. Contradicting {the SS} or pleading for mercy was out of the question; the mere instinct of self-preservation warned our leaders to keep still. By 1944 they had reached the limit of their endurance. Edelstein, Zucker, Gruenberger, the Prague Council of Elders, Eppstein, the Council of Elders of the German Jews, as a group posed only one question, one desperate, courageous question when once again they were called to headquarters for another transport. {"How many more?"} The answer they received was "auf weisung" (as directed) {and they went} into the selfsame transport. Auf weisung meant the unequivocal death sentence in the directive, to be executed by shooting or gassing upon arrival. Thus our leaders disappeared into the insatiable inferno of extermination.

I have anticipated the end of the Council of Elders by selection. It actually happened much later, shortly before the end of the war, when I already had been sent on a transport. I only learned of the events described above upon my return from Auschwitz.

It can be safely assumed that the Council of Elders, as {did} all of us in the ghetto, believed the lying, malicious assurances of the SS at the headquarters that the eastbound transports were merely resettlement to new Jewish ghettos awaiting them or to be built by them. We believed these deceptions because we wanted to believe them. Man hopes and hopes and deceives himself as long as there flickers one spark of life in him and as long as nothing is proven to the contrary.

When our loved ones and friends were torn from our side by the transports to the East, they would take with them stamped postcards or letters that they were supposed to throw from the train during the long journey, or take a chance in throwing them to some "civilian" or railwayman at some stops. We agreed on code words containing geographic information or warnings in phrases and words only we should understand. Of the thousands of those deported, a few messages miraculously reached their destinations. After being decoded the messages confirmed our worst fears in spite of the strictest secrecy demanded by the Council of Elders who tried to avoid the rising fear and panic of everyone.

After a few months {of transports} the Council of Elders knew of the activities in the East, but they said nothing. They even knew of how little value the so-called "protection" of the AK1 and AK2 was.

Like all of us they hoped that the war would end at an earlier date, before we would all be swallowed up in the endless expanse of the East. As for the rest of us, we knew nothing; we heard rumors that we did not want to believe, we hoped, we practiced self-deception. We desperately searched for protection and security for our families—up to the last transport. The eastbound transports represented our eternal scourge of oppressive fear. Transports {to Theresienstadt} came from all parts of Central Europe; all {outgoing} transports left only for the East. It was obvious that Theresienstadt was merely the transfer point.

I have purposely described extensively the terror-laden atmosphere in times of transport to explain the effect of its horrors on us more clearly: interrupted by short periods in which we could take a hopeful breath. Perhaps {we thought} this was the last transport. {This also explains} our increasing demoralization, the gradual loss of our humanity, our ethical principles, our compassion.

I recall one of the days when the SS car from Prague or Berlin with the "birds of death," Eichmann or Möhs, pulled up at the headquarters when a new transport was commanded. The Council of Elders assembled for the usual continuous day and night conference to make up the transport list; deadline—two days. For the umpteenth time my by then widowed sister Ida was once more "in the transport": that is, she had received a slip of paper with her name and her number for the transport from the room elder. She hurried desperately to my place to inform me of the fateful news. I rush immediately to Era Kohn, my boss, on whose list both Ida and I have been placed; he advises me to try to reach Edelstein, Zucker, and Gruenberger immediately and ask them for her exemption.

The Magdeburger barracks, our central office, is very well guarded; no admittance for unauthorized persons. I am one of the authorized ones, and I have a permanent permit. I know the way to the private apartments of the Council of Elders, all of them my former "clients." Normally the wives, who know me well, are at home. A short note with the presentation of the slip with the name and number of my sister together with my last name is enough. I am assured that their husbands will find the slip with the unspoken plea under their plate during their dinner and will protect her.

This procedure took place at least twelve to fifteen times up to the moment when I myself was unexpectedly included {in a transport} for having been a participant and victim of the "Painters' Affair"; more of that later. Ida, weak, old, defenseless, helpless, who had lost my protection, was put on the next list and disappeared in the maw of a transport to the East.

(I have interrupted this report for a few months. I am continuing {now} during a few quiet rainy days of my vacation in Vienna, early January of 1977.)

6

RATIONS AND THE SCHLEUSE

The daily ration {consisted of}: mornings—ersatz coffee without sugar, one-half loaf of black bread, which represented the mainstay of our diet, the main source of calories; at noon—a weak soup containing no fat with some white turnips, called *wrucken*, with a disagreeable taste, cooked with leaves, sand, and dirt, sometimes with a trace of flour {for thickening}. Sometimes there was lentil soup for a change made from dried ground lentil pods, gray, tasteless, unappealing, stinking water without any nutritional value; normally we would throw it out disgustedly until we found regular takers for it: old people.

That group had a hard time {trying} to avoid starvation. They could not do any hard work, and the children as well as the people doing heavy physical labor needed more calories and had to be fed better. The SS, however, doled out our daily rations of calories according to a head count; we therefore had to give larger portions to the workers, smaller portions to the children and the sick, and minimal rations to the poor old people. The old ones were in a desperate situation; they starved. The rations had little nutritional value and did not satisfy their hunger. Thus, whenever we would stand in line at any of the seven kitchens with our tin bowls, we would immediately be surrounded by groups of the elderly who would ask humbly: "Are you taking your soup?" They were eager customers for the so-called lentil soup; it was a pitiful sight. Their weight loss was visibly rapid, and they died like flies: enfeebled, demoralized, tired—an unforgettable sight.

After the soup at noon we would receive one potato, unpeeled, or sometimes peeled. The cooks would throw the peels, called šlupky, on a heap behind the kitchens, where they would be picked up {by the garbage detail} later. But they began to ferment and stink before being taken away. Clusters of old people would crowd around these heaps and would pull out the thickest peels to put into their bowls. They would gnaw off any potato left in the peel or would try to make soup from the peels. Eating the šlupkys without cooking them would have the worst consequences. {The old people} would come down with diarrhea, unstoppable enteritis; they had to go to the hospital—miserable, stinking barracks—where they were poorly nursed and quite literally "shit out" their lives in the latrines. A horrible chapter.

Married couples had a somewhat better chance, because they had

Elderly person climbing to attic quarters.
(Courtesy Leo Baeck Institute)

someone who would try to provide for them, keep them clean, and supplement their meager nutrition with items they saved from their own small rations. That was the way my brother-in-law Julius died, then my aunt Fritzi from Vienna, and later my brother Ernst, who had been weakened to the point that he {became infected with} one disease after another. His wife Stella survived him. She worked very hard in one of the kitchens. After I had left Theresienstadt, she was put into a transport. Her eldest son, Ludwig, a splendidly strong young man of about twenty-two or twenty-three {actually he was in his late twenties at the time} had seen service with the Czech dragoons and was now a member of the Ghetto Guard, our police force. No sidearms, civilian clothing, a black cap with a yellow band, and a cape: that was their uniform. He lost his life in a tragic manner.

The Ghetto Guard does not take themselves very seriously, just as we do not take them very seriously. They are powerless, without weapons; they are only a small group, without any real authority, who normally guarded warehouses and who stood around when new transports arrived, supposedly to prevent looting during the *schleuse* (channel).

Here I would like to explain the cursed activity of the *schleuse*. Every person on the transport who arrived in Theresienstadt from the outside was loaded down with suitcases, bundles, soft luggage such as pillows, featherbeds, down quilts, etc. They seemed to have prepared for some type of Siberian winter—how fearfully clairvoyant—with hiking boots, ski suits, fur coats, fur hats, foodstuff, linens, cooking utensils, herbs, spices, etc.

Those who did not collapse on the way from Bauschowitz, the railroad station for the ghetto, arrived at the Jaeger barracks bathed in perspiration. The Jaeger barracks was not actually a barracks but a fortress casemate, a subterranean vault made of bricks and stone, with two barred windows and an entrance gate. Otherwise it was simply a damp dungeon, its stone floor covered with nothing but excelsior. . . . [After the newcomers had been relieved of their luggage and it had been immediately cleaned out of all valuables, everyone searched for his rucksack, marked with his name and transport number from among the heap of nearly empty suitcases and rucksacks thrown higgledy-piggledy. {They} all stretched out, deadly tired, on the excelsior covering the stone floors of the casemate, resigned to {their} fate.]¹ The most elegant ladies—and there were many of them— the most self-assured gentlemen, when they were ready to leave the Jaeger barracks upon being assigned to the labor force, would leave the place broken, deeply shaken, frequently crying.

They would enter the vault dressed more or less properly, apprehensive, respectable burghers, ladies, small businessmen, professionals, well-groomed children, young men and girls, sometimes subdued, sometimes unruly, etc. Two days later they all looked alike, gray, decrepit, unwashed (there were no washrooms in the Jaeger barracks), covered from head to toe with excelsior scraps, unshaven, smelly. They had been registered, counted, and recounted {and had} undergone a cursory medical examination. A few wooden tubs with soup, potatoes and pieces of bread floating in it, had been brought to them on a cart. This was their introduction to the ghetto food that was to be their daily fare until their death or until their transport to the East. The two days in the schleuse represented a kind of quarantine.

In the meantime, their luggage was "processed," that is, it was subjected to the schleuse routine. Not one piece of luggage belonging to any newcomer escaped this procedure. At the departure point, where the victims had been loaded into freight trains, every piece of luggage had to be marked clearly with the transport number, home address, and name of owner. Upon arrival the luggage and its owner were parted. The owner continued to the schleuse in the Jaeger barracks, the luggage to a nearby hut where it was thrown on a large pile. Along one side of the hut large tables were set

Man in the schleuse.
(Courtesy Leo Baeck Institute)

up. Behind these tables stood the young members of the Ghetto Guard who had really no other function but as underlings.

The Czech gendarmes were the actual supervisory personnel with authority. And the berušky: they were female inmates, wearing the Jewish star, of course, like every Jew in {Theresienstadt}.[2] The job of the berušky was to pick up from the pile of luggage bundle by bundle, suitcase after suitcase, all the soft luggage and throw it on the tables, break it open, take out nearly three-quarters of the contents, and sort it into separate piles. Amazing, the way they did this: featherbeds, woolen blankets, men's and women's underwear and clothes, food, toothbrushes, mouthwash, soap especially, house slippers, spices, mustard jars, everything, everything, was taken out. This procedure of systematically robbing the defenseless, imprisoned Jews of their last few belongings was called schleusen, and from that time on it has become part of the German language.

All inmates, without exception, had to submit to this process, the main purpose of which was to "liberate" gold and valuables. {The Germans} hardly ever found anything of value {because} in spite of all that, there was enough gold and currency that was so well hidden, so unobtrusive, that even the cleverest, most ruthless Gestapo men and gendarmes failed to find anything. An enumeration of the hiding places could probably fill a separate chapter that would be amusing. In the context of this sad chronicle of human cruelty and human suffering, however, it is meaningless.

The heaps of odds and ends, minus the items stolen and sorted by articles, even candlesticks, matchboxes, toothpaste, brushes, combs, lighters, were then sorted for their quality and distributed. All the better clothing, shoes, featherbeds, pillows, and blankets would be repackaged, and after the SS had stolen the best items, the remainder would be sent to the bombed-out cities of Germany. Second and third choice went into the ghetto warehouses for possible local use. The rest, the odds and ends, the half-squeezed tubes of toothpaste, lanolin, other kinds of ointments, the candle stubs, the flashlights minus their batteries, matchboxes, mouth-wash, pencil stubs, erasers, notebooks, writing paper, and thousands of other useless items, rubbish, were sent as merchandise to the "stores" of the ghetto, where we were allowed to purchase them for bogus money, the ghetto currency. The ghetto bank paid those fictional bank notes to the working inhabitants of the ghetto. They would purchase nothing more than the sad refuse, passing for merchandise in our "stores." The Red Cross Commission was impressed.

I have dwelled to a greater extent in this chapter on "schleusen" because it represented such an integral part of the life in Theresienstadt. There was no inhabitant of the town who had not passed through this process, who had not been robbed and finally separated from his last few belongings. The same procedure in Auschwitz was called kanada.

7

THE FATE OF MY FAMILY

For a description of life in Theresienstadt during the years 1941–44, I will combine my own experiences with the fate of my immediate family as well as that of dear friends, men and women alike. I can reconstruct my own life practically day by day with the help of hundreds of sketches that have been saved through a unique stroke of luck—in spite of incarceration in the Little Fortress and my subsequent transport to Auschwitz. All my brothers and sisters and their children have passed through Theresienstadt with the exception of my brother Karl, his wife Vilma, with their sons Herbert and George, who all managed to escape to the West, as well as the youngest son of my brother Ernst, Hans. Only Dora Perlhefter, the daughter of my favorite sister, Alice, a widow, and I, the youngest of the siblings, have survived. None of my {other} siblings nor my wife of that time[1] were as dear to me as my beloved Alice, Nono {nickname for Doris Rauch}, and {Alice's} late husband Artur who had died at such an early age (forty-six years old).

One day, my sister Ida Bunzl-Federn, her husband Julius, and their two daughters Marianne and Hanne arrived in Theresienstadt with one of the Prague transports. My brother-in-law Julius was in his late seventies at the time, sickly and terrified. He had always been a true Prague aesthete, part of the German cultural circle, and could hardly speak Czech. He was a composer and virtuoso manqué who played the piano enchantingly. He was completely unworldly but had to pursue a commercial career, for which he had neither talent, inclination, nor training. His commercial pursuits had catastrophic results, making my sister's dowry disappear into thin air. But he was a charming, lovable man, twenty years my sister's senior, tall, with a red {beard} à la Ruebezahl {German fairy-tale character known for his red beard}, and no one failed to notice him on the daily promenade along the Graben {one of the main streets in the center of Prague}. His wife and children adored him. Even when they lived in straitened circumstances after his many failures, their numerous friends continued to gather at their apartment because of the warm, friendly atmosphere at "the Bunzls."

The daughters refused to marry because they were so happy at home. Whenever my mother, Cilly, would visit them in Prague, she would come back laughing and shaking her head. She would say: "They live a hand-to-mouth existence, but I have never seen a happier, more satisfied, joyful, music-loving household than at the Bunzls." They were all idealists, well read, musical, artistic, and carefree, unworldly, and trusting. But even in the happiest families critical events can rattle the firmest foundations; in the case of Julius, they threatened almost financial ruin that could only be prevented with the help of the family. Julius, the best, most solid, honest, and in business, the most ill-equipped, untalented person in the world, had an idée fixe. He invented a "musical notation typewriter" to record his and other so-called composers' works. However, he had only the idea, no technical training whatsoever, no mechanical aptitude, no manual dexterity. He was only an inventor.

He gave the commission to a cheating so-called "mechanic," Ocenášek—his name became anathema in the family—who swindled them out of the dowry of my sister Ida without having produced the promised model of the machine that was needed to register the patent. Another "expert" at least produced some mechanical blueprints. These blueprints apparently remained Julius's idée fixe for the rest of his life, which I had not known.

He was already quite old when he arrived in Theresienstadt, but still slim and straight; his Ruebezahl beard had turned white. Like most old people in Theresienstadt he soon contracted enteritis, the form of diarrhea frequently deadly for the elderly. He was moved into one of the block sickrooms, where I visited him. He was so weak, so emaciated, obviously dying, his beard untrimmed. He asked me to remove a packet of papers from under his pillow. I opened it—it contained the blueprints of his cloud cuckooland musical notation typewriter. "Guard them well, my life's work is in them. I know that one day the plans will become reality, only I shall not see it anymore." Two days later he was dead. The blueprints disappeared when I was sent to the Little Fortress.

(Again I have interrupted the writing for a while, for a vacation in Vienna. A year has passed since. Another vacation, March–April 1978. The vacation will be over come April 4, and my life will probably end as well sooner or later. Therefore I must hurry to finish this disagreeable, often dramatic chapter, the years in the concentration camp. I write in Vienna on a cool, gray day, in my comfortable little apartment on Modena Square.)

I do not recall the precise date of the arrival {of Ernest and his family} in the spring of 1942. Ernst was in his mid-sixties at the time. He was normally a bit stout, and like every one of us he too very quickly lost about fifty to sixty pounds because of the unaccustomed diet.

This chapter also relates directly to the sad ending of {his son}, my nephew, Ludwig, whom I have mentioned earlier. The sequence of events was as follows, and this individual example can be representative of hundreds of cases where young people unjustly and because of ludicrous trifles, jealousies, envy, viciousness, cruelties, and meanness simply disappeared.

The previously mentioned Ghetto Guard was originally loosely organized; to avoid thefts, their main duty was to make sure that no one was on the street after curfew without a permit. Otherwise they did their guard duty only in the barracks. The guards accompanying the new transports from the train into the ghetto were provided from their ranks.

During the schleusen procedure they were there to prevent the stolen merchandise from disappearing into the beruškys' pockets, especially cigarettes and tobacco. They in turn were watched by the Czech gendarmes. The gendarmes, of course, stole like magpies, only smaller items, naturally without any protest from the Ghetto Guards or the beruškys. A few of the Ghetto Guards enjoyed the confidence and often unspoken secret assistance of the gendarmes.

My nephew, having served with the Pardubitzer Dragoons, knew the typically military jargon and had an almost chummy relationship with some of the Czech gendarmes. One summer evening, I believe it was in 1943, the Ghetto Guards were on schleusen duty for a new transport. One of his gendarme friends put a few small items in {Ludwig's} pocket, without his noticing it. What {were they}? A candle stub, a box of matches, a half-used piece of soap, that was all. Having finished work around midnight, Ludwig returned to his sentry quarters through the blacked-out streets.

Suddenly, a flashlight glared in his face, and he was ordered to stop. "Control, hands up, body search." This was no SS man, no gendarme, but another Ghetto Guard who fancied himself to be of higher rank than Ludwig and who searched Ludwig's pockets and confiscated the candle, matches, and soap. Good-naturedly, Ludwig asked him what a fellow guardsman was doing searching his pockets. The answer was: "I am going to report you." "Are you crazy?" said Ludwig. "Denouncing a fellow Jew?" "That's my business," was the answer.

Ludwig, being a good-looking, tall young man, always in high spirits, was very popular with the love-starved women and girls of Theresienstadt without giving much thought to his successes. Among others he enjoyed the favors of a girl from Prague, a sweet girl, no great beauty, who was courted in vain by another Ghetto Guard. Ludwig was not aware of any of that, and in his blind jealous rage the rival stalked Ludwig, because he probably knew the gendarmes would have passed him something. The damnable traitor did indeed denounce Ludwig to the commandant of the Ghetto Guard, but in his viciousness he sent a copy of the report directly to the so-called chief of police . . . whose story will be told later.

The report reached the assistant commandant, Dr. Bass from Brünn, who, of course, was well acquainted with Ludwig and was very kindly disposed toward him.[2] He immediately tore up the denunciation and had the denunciator report to him, asking him what was he thinking of. "Here we only do our duty and reject any attempts at personal revenge. This is against regulations." The man received three nights extra duty as punishment. With this everyone thought the affair was ended.

Three days later Ludwig received a note, an "official notice": "Ghetto Guardsman Ludwig Troller is being assigned to the next transport with special instructions as punishment for theft." This order hit us like a ton of bricks. Within minutes the whole ghetto had heard of it, and since everyone knew him, his superiors and protectors tried to save him. "With special instructions" meant death by firing squad after arrival in the East.

The above chain of events brings us to the worst criminal of all the ghetto inhabitants, the commandant of the Ghetto Guards, who bore the title he had given himself, "chief of police." He was a thoroughly notorious figure by the name of Loewenstein.[3]

He had appeared one day in Theresienstadt as an individual prisoner being delivered to the then-existing ghetto prison. The chief jailer was an old friend of mine, Ing. Josef Maendl. Local rumors as well as reports had it that {Loewenstein} was visited in prison by two SS bigwigs. Then it was rumored that he supposedly had been a Prussian lieutenant commander in the German navy who had been found to have a Jewish grandmother in his family tree.[4] This, of course, caused him to be cashiered and to be transported to Theresienstadt. Whether any of this is true, I do not know. After a few days he was let out of prison and was assigned special housing.

On another day a note from headquarters to the ghetto administration informed them that the Jew Loewenstein had been named head of the Ghetto Guards and would assume his duties immediately. The Council of Elders was rather surprised. And so the great unknown Prussian, the Jew Loewenstein, took over the Ghetto Guards and began a tight reorganization. Drills, standing at attention, saluting, marching, passing in review, in short: "the works." Then, pompously, he drilled his innocent, unarmed boys according to the Prussian drill order: to assemble, fall out in formation, platoons (there were not enough of them to form companies), and finally to parade in goose step, and then he invited the SS staff for a demonstration. They came, were amazed, turned pale, and the next morning there appeared the following notation in the daily orders: Drilling, marching, or any kind of formation exercises are strictly forbidden. The captain was severely reprimanded. "Did he think that he was creating the nucleus of a Jewish Praetorian Guard? One never knows with these Jewish pigs, does one?"

For about a week he kept very quiet and in the background. He even got married in a rabbinically sanctioned ghetto ceremony to the daughter of Ing. Pollak from Brünn who had owned a large heating and furnace establishment and whom I knew well professionally.

That is all for now about the captain, our "chief of police." Let us return to the "special order" of the captain regarding my nephew. Like aroused hornets—without stings—all his friends and relatives tried to rescind the fatal order. Stella, Ludwig's mother, weeping, rushed into the office of the chief without any introduction, only a desperate mother begging on her knees for Ludwig's life. The answer was: A crime committed on duty must be severely punished; sorry. {Ludwig's} immediate superior, Dr. Bass, tried, by citing the regulations, to make it clear that such trifling matters did not merit the most severe punishment, that is, death. He fought patiently and devotedly for, as he said, his best, most disciplined man in vain. Then I approached {Loewenstein} with two helpers whom, in my opinion, he could not resist. I spoke with Loewenstein's wife, who had also gone to school with Ludwig, the daughter of Ing. Pollak from Brünn. The second person was Ing. Zucker of the Council of Elders, the secretary of labor. After I had made sure that Ing. Zucker, as well as the captain's wife, had spoken to him, I also went to his office.

I stated my plea calmly, pointed to Ludwig's blameless record until now, his excellent military behavior, and the minor importance of the items found on him, and finally I pointed out the fact that it was the jealous act of a vengeful fellow Guardsman. The answer, militarily concise: "I have made my decision. The chief of police must preserve discipline. I cannot rescind a decision once made; sorry." I was devastated.

All efforts had been frustrated by the Prussian intransigence and arrogance of a foreign {Loewenstein was born in Minsk}, notorious, and un-feeling person, whose background was known to no one but the SS. Of course, Ludwig was assigned to the transport, and thus a young man, full of hope and promise, my nephew, perished helplessly in the flower of his youth. It was a stroke of "luck" that his father, Ernst, my brother, had died of general debility {earlier}. His widow, Stella, was left behind, almost completely shattered after the loss of her husband and her oldest son within such a brief span of time.

Only the second son, Fritz, who had begun his studies in medicine before entering the ghetto and who served in the health department of the ghetto, remained to her. Fritz was tall like his brother, slim, blond, with a noble, friendly manner; an intellectual, complex person.

He served in several area medical centers in the same capacity, as an intern in a hospital. He had a good heart, unlike many of his colleagues, worked hard at the profession, which he hoped to continue after peace had come again. I do not know what fate befell him and his mother. They still were in the camp when I was being deported with the painters' group.

The last relative remaining to be mentioned is the youngest son of my brother Ernst, Hans. During the war he worked in the textile industry in Huddersfield, Yorkshire. He had started studying textile engineering be-fore leaving home. A few years after the war he emigrated to Montreal, Canada, where he got married. He was not very successful in his work at the start. However, this situation improved considerably when he worked as a carpenter, paperhanger, and renovator of antique furniture in the United States. His last known address was Mountain View, California. To-tally unexpectedly and without any obvious reason, he committed suicide in California. Why? For what reason? {He was} an exceedingly decent, proud, and sensitive man, a healthy fifty years old. I still mourn him today. With his death the once-so-powerful line of my brother Ernst died out.

I already described the fate of my sister Ida and her husband Julius. . . . {Their} daughter, Marianne, single and somewhat advanced in age, had no way of remaining in Theresienstadt since I could only protect her mother, not my nephews and nieces.

The second daughter, Hanne, was tall and rather thin with a pale, freckled face, like her father; quite pretty and candid. She wore large glasses. She was very musical, totally unselfish, and her only concern was the welfare of her music students. She had been highly regarded in the Prague Jewish community for her sociable and humane attitude {and was} well loved, especially by the children.

Everyone being deported from the cities to Theresienstadt thought only of his own well-being and stuffed his luggage with as much food as he could carry—the food of course was *geschleust*—meaning stolen out of the luggage; he never saw it again. Hanne, however, had a small rucksack with her few belongings and one box, which managed to pass the schleuse untouched thanks to the intervention of the gendarmes. It was full to the brim with notebooks, drawing paper, colored pencils, pencils, paintbrushes—everything for the children in our children's home. She was well known to everyone of the Council of Elders and therefore was put immediately on a protection list.

Hanne was sickly but with a very strong will. She began immediately to work with the children in the children's home, to draw and sing with them. Only in her off-hours would she visit her dying father. She never complained, she was under the care of a physician, and she had brought a small supply of special pills with her to the ghetto. That supply, however, ran out after a while, and there was no way to replace it. Her strength diminished visibly, {but} she forced herself with great effort to work. From her mother I learned the cause of her sudden decline. She suffered from lymphogranulomatosis, an incurable type of blood cancer. She died shortly after the death of her father.

About my favorite sister, Alice, a widow at the time, and her daughter, Dora, I have already written. Saying farewell to them, first in Brünn, and then the traumatic shock of seeing both of them assigned to an eastbound transport just a few {months} after having found them again in Theresienstadt was a devastating shock to me. There was no way I could help them.

Again I had to say good-bye to those whom I loved most of my family. I had great difficulty recuperating from this desperate, deep depression. I can do nothing more than sketch their fate in the East. After the end of the war Dora found out that I had survived also. The contact was soon reestablished, and we were happy to find each other again. Shortly after that Dora emigrated to New York City, and I followed her in 1948. Our rebirth, her being here (in the sense of being alive), has made the bonds between us all the stronger. We are continually in touch, she is my anchor—my "security blanket"—a daughter, I might say, who after the heavy losses of the Nazi period represents family and continuity for me.

My brother Karl, his wife Vilma, and their sons Herbert and George left Vienna, their home, in time and after many adventures, via Brussels, France, and {Portugal}, arrived in the United States. Herbert served in the {British} Army and George was a G.I. in the U.S. Army. Karl and Vilma, who had returned to Vienna and lived in a senior citizens' home, died there at a ripe old age. Herbert lives in London with his wife Eva and his daughter Monica; George lives in Paris with his wife Kirsten, their little daughter Tonka, and Fenn, his daughter from a previous marriage. Thus far the fate of the house of Ludwig and Caccilie Troller, and what the war and the Nazis have done to us. I consider it good fortune that my mother died before all that. At the beginning of the war there was: Ernst, Stella, Ludwig, Fritz, Grete (she died of leukemia in 1936), Hans; Ida, Julius, Marianne, Hanne; Karl, Vilma, Herbert, George; Alice, Doris; Norbert. Total—seventeen persons: one died normally; nine, concentration camp victims; seven, survivors.

8

LIFE IN THE GHETTO

In th{is} next chapter I want to describe my life with my group at work and the ghetto life in general. {It was} a tightly knit unit, quite well organized, totally without freedom, "subhumans" (I know of no better expression) as they called us, without rights, doomed without realizing it, and hoping that it would be us who survived. When I arrived in the {spring of 1942} we passed through the schleuse and, with few of our possessions left, were assigned new quarters.

{There was} complete separation of families. Men were sent to the Sudeten barracks, a large, three-story building at the periphery of the town. It had been a storehouse for uniforms; that is, it consisted mostly of storerooms of large dimensions, a modern concrete building. The rooms were totally bare; naked light bulbs hung here and there from the ceiling; {there were} concrete floors, barred windows. Everywhere three-tiered bunks, nailed together, with mattresses filled with excelsior and pillows of the same kind.

Later on we built little tables and stools from stolen leftover wood. On one side there was a large courtyard, our exercise place where we usually met in groups, mostly people from the same town. On the ground floor, accessible from the yard, there was a large kitchen, a typical military installation, metal stoves, pots, mixing machines, and kettles. The soup and the potatoes would be poured into wooden tubs and vats that stood around a serving table.

Behind the table the mostly female kitchen personnel handed out the food with large ladles. People lined up in long lines on the other side of the table with a bowl, spoon, and fork until they arrived at the head of the line, to have food ladled into their bowl. There was no need for a knife; only rarely was there something like meat that would need cutting, and it would be served in bite size. For the noon meal we usually received turnip soup followed by a medium-sized potato, no fat whatsoever. Weekly rations were a thin sliver of margarine, five centimeters long. A {fraction of a} loaf of bread was distributed daily in the barracks either before or after the workday. The rations were very strictly regulated.

For breakfast there was black, unsweetened, ersatz coffee, the same in the evening. Our only substantial calories were the bread and the single potato. From time to time (once every two weeks) we would receive a yeast dumpling, which was very tasty, but which exhausted our margarine

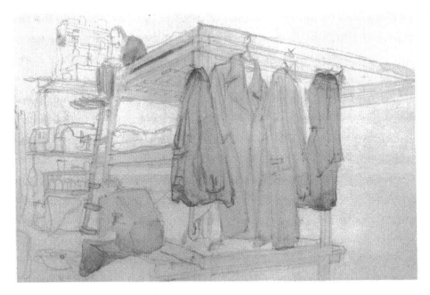

Sudeten barracks: three-tiered bunks.
(Courtesy Leo Baeck Institute)

and sugar rations by having to use them to help the dumpling slide down. The dumpling was delicious, but one hour later our stomachs were growling with hunger for more.

The women, separated from the men, were housed in the {Hamburger and Dresdner} barracks. These barracks had been Austrian infantry barracks from the time of Empress Maria Theresa. They were gigantic, three-story buildings, covering an entire block, with high, steep roofs. Their size and layout were rather impressive. The individual floors had vaulted ceilings. The rectangular plan of the building included two to three gigantic courtyards surrounded by arcades. These open arcades formed the corridors that led to the lodgings, mostly large rooms, a few larger halls. Every lodging had windows facing the street. Everything there was easy to keep an eye on, and in winter the arcade-surrounded courtyards were icy cold.

Line-up for food.
(Courtesy Leo Baeck Institute)

Some of the larger rooms had large tiled cooking stoves that were in
almost constant use. At every corner of the square there was a staircase
and washrooms with faucets and wash basins. Most people used their
bowls {to wash in} after having drunk their coffee from them. During the
summer months after work the arcades were used by people for sitting
outdoors on little stools or on the banister and visiting with their friends
and neighbors. The courtyards themselves were always crowded. Here
people lined up for rations—their children played ball or soccer—fetched
bread, delivered coal; there people stood in a tight circle around a coffin,
a funeral. Perhaps in one corner—after work—a lecture; in another corner, in the second courtyard, a group of singers accompanied by a guitar,
or a choral group, a theater performance during the summer, etc.

Dresdner barracks courtyard.
(Courtesy Leo Baeck Institute)

The women in their barracks had no wooden bedsteads; the vaulted ceilings there were too low. They spread their excelsior-filled mattresses one next to the other on the floor, which left only a small space to climb into bed. The blanket and pillow at the top end would be rolled up; at the foot end the inevitable little stool that served as a table as well.

{The women} stood patiently in line at the stove with their little pots until it was their turn. The stove was heated with paper, rolled up and wetted down, then air-dried again, with whatever wood chips they could find. They also made use of a clever ghetto invention: a cut-up tin can (as in "canned food" can) with a few holes punched in the sides, a few wires

Courtyard concert: audience.
(Courtesy Leo Baeck Institute)

put through the holes at the bottom; on the side, a slit; for heating material, snips of paper and matches. It was amazing how fast this contraption
could heat up soup or coffee. Every one of the women's lodgings was
spotlessly clean.[1]

The women did the same work as the men, with the exception of su-
pervisors and "toilet guards." Wherever there were toilets in a building,
individual ones or common latrines, there was a washbasin on a stand at
the door, and everyone, without exception, had to wash his hands after
using the toilet to prevent infectious diseases. The toilet guards watched
that no one evaded this duty.

What good were all these elaborate cooking preparations? Wherever
there are women, there will be cooking, even with practically nothing, as

Courtyard concert: performers.
(Courtesy Leo Baeck Institute)

in the ghetto. The main purpose of this was the following: after the families had been split up, separated, the men in the Sudeten barracks, the
women in the Dresdner and Hamburger barracks, the children in the
children's homes (the former local schools), the commandant issued permission, after I believe six to eight months, that families could reunite for
a few hours daily in the women's barracks. Thus the Dresdner and Hamburger barracks after 5:30 in the evening resembled a beehive.

Imagine, if you will, one husband and several children seated around
tightly packed straw sacks and being served supper on the little stool from

their bowls. It would have been a funny sight if it were not so admirable and sad at the same time. There is no one so sacrificing or ready to make sacrifices as a mother. She will save her rations; usually the husband would also bring some food he had saved. She has a little pot, or a bowl, and concocts something tasty: "ghetto cake" made from dry breadcrumbs, coffee with grounds, saved sugar, or saccharin, or *penezeln*, paper-thin slices of toasted bread, with or without margarine, with garlic, or slices of toasted bread with a dusting of powdered sugar.

Then there were the salads and spinach, made from all sorts of weeds—dandelion if in season. And the many kinds of potato preparations without butter. Between 6:00 and 7:00 in the evening such a women's lodging crowded with men, women, children, squatting on the floor, closely pressed together but orderly, resembled a Turkish coffeehouse after Ramadan fasts.

The situation threatened to become critical before the family visits in the women's barracks were finally permitted. There was complete separation of families. The husbands tried every trick in the book to get in touch with their wives. They would see each other only through the barred windows of the ground floor, and you can imagine the conversation, women tightly pressed together at every window with their husbands equally tightly pressed together on the outside.

Men searched for and found all kinds of ways to enter the women's barracks. They paid the cleaning or supply crews with their cigarettes or their bread rations to let them take their place. In the morning there were the milk, coal, bread, and supply crews; at noon the kitchen-cleaning crews, the corpse collectors, etc. It was a common sight to see the columns of longing husbands with their milk cans or coal sacks waiting in front of the barracks gate to be let in by the gendarme gatekeeper. Barely inside the court there was the lightning delivery of the goods {they brought} to cellar or kitchen; they joined the waiting women and within minutes had disappeared without a trace into cubicles, storerooms, coal bins so as not to waste one precious minute with the loved ones, because twenty to thirty minutes later they had to assemble anew at the gate to be checked and to leave. The coal-blackened backs of the ladies did not attract too much attention. The phenomenon of the coal-blackened backside was accepted with a smile or sometimes with envy or regret.

To begin with, the men were concentrated in the gigantic Sudeten barracks, as I mentioned before. This was a lodging for a multitude of people, with a constant buzzing noise that needed getting used to, a coming and going day and night, conversations, the rattle of tin bowls preventing any semblance of quiet, undisturbed sleep. [Over 6,000 men lived in the gigantic storerooms, 100 to 300 in a room.] The body emanations, the smell of sweat of hundreds of working men who seldom had a chance to bathe— one could not overcome this even with open windows. It was . . . nauseating. It stank. Men also lived in the smaller barracks, the Hannover, the Gendarmerie, etc.

The Magdeburger barracks was the office building of the ghetto, the government and administrative center. It resembled the other large barracks with its spacious courtyards. The main gate featured white, square stone on black-painted outer walls. The keystone above the gate featured two horse heads crossed. One or two Ghetto Guards flanked the gates.

All offices were contained there. The Council of Elders—seven in number—had their privileged apartments there, one to two rooms each. The drafting office, the center of official statistics and secret artistic activity, was under the guidance of the highly talented "Fritta." I was good friends with some of the men: Peter Kien, Aussenberg,[2] Fritta. Some of their names I have forgotten. I will have more to say about this group later on in the chapter on the "Painters' Affair." The Magdeburger—this office-building barracks—also contained a kitchen, supply rooms, and workshops.

The engineering department where I worked had a fairly large drafting

Magdeburger barracks main gate.
(Courtesy Leo Baeck Institute)

hall in the Hannover barracks, catercorner from the Magdeburger. The head of the department was the previously mentioned young architect from Prague, Era Kohn, a confirmed Communist, very talented, of great integrity, and ruthless, but an unshakable protector of his crew of architects and engineers whom he had plucked out of the many transports. It was one of the best-run departments in Theresienstadt.

There were also small subdepartments that I cannot describe extensively because I came only rarely in contact with them: the waterworks, the power plant, the health service, the street cleaning, agriculture, and others, [and] six or seven kitchen installations.

One of the ramparts with its vaulted casemates was enlarged, warehouses added to it, forming the complex of the former garrison bakery, now the ghetto bakery. Jewish professional bakers worked there under the direction of experienced [members of] AK1 and AK2. {The bakers} took over existing small rooms where they had spacious living quarters {that were} warm and had privacy. As an architect who had furnished their quarters, I was often a guest there. I did this, of course, as a sideline after working hours, altogether separate from my work in the engineering department.

I also painted and sketched the bakers frequently. These sketches would often be bought by the bakers and paid for with one-half a loaf of bread. Furnishing a room was paid for with two loaves of bread or twenty cigarettes. These customers were well-to-do. Cigarettes and bread, margarine and sugar, were the common coin of the ghetto. Sixteen cigarettes was the equivalent of a loaf of bread.

Among other ghetto installations was the bauhof in which experienced carpenters and cabinetmakers worked. The director of the lumberyard was Langer, a lumber expert, the son-in-law of my cousin in Pilsen. He survived the war also {and} emigrated to New South Wales in Australia where he was extremely successful in producing prefab housing.

Ghetto bakery.
(*Courtesy Leo Baeck Institute*)

The scraps and sometimes even whole boards from this lumberyard would disappear nightly from there and served as the raw material for our stools, chairs, wall-shelving, and other improvised everyday items. The main job of the lumberyard was the production of slat beds, one, two, or three story–high bedsteads that housed the . . . thousands of ghetto inhabitants. It also produced the new latrines, storage and sleeping barracks, a modern children's home, a music pavilion, and numerous new buildings for office space, all covered with pasteboard roofing.

A large part of the daily life took place in the courtyards and galleries. The barracks were all the same height, so that the gables would not show over the grass-covered walls of the ramparts. All of them had a first, second, and third floor topped off with high attics recently covered with

"Jedermann" ("Everyman") performance.
(Courtesy Leo Baeck Institute)

red-dotted plain tile. These attics, previously neglected and dirty with accumulations of decades-old dust and soot, became an important, integral part of the barracks.

Previously unused, we now converted them—after a thorough cleaning—for our purposes. Since there were no wall partitions in the attic, only wooden beams and support rafters, large spaces were created with slanted walls of considerable height lit by a few skylights. They {provided} the only possibility for housing, albeit primitive housing, for the great masses of newly arrived thousands flowing in by transport from Czechoslovakia, Austria, and the Reich. In the unoccupied attic spaces unforgettable concerts, dramas, and operas were performed.[3]

The remaining space in the L and Q {longitudinal and cross} streets was taken up by ordinary townhouses, mostly dating back to the time of Maria Theresa with here and there some new or renovated smaller houses. On the average these houses had a main floor and a second floor; all had high roofs. There were perhaps two dozen old-fashioned stores in the streets around the parade ground. In the yard of two houses in a side street was a typical garrison brothel with tiny rooms without any plumbing on two floors fronted by open balconies. These quarters were choice housing for the *prominente*.[4]

The health department developed a plan to improve the health of the town because the great threat of a typhus epidemic lurked in the foreseeable future. The department of pest control was [expanded]; requests for disinfectants were increased. The architectural department planned what is known . . . as "renovation to eliminate overcrowding of inner cities," a new field of science.

Every single house in every block originally had a courtyard. In the course of the 200 years since Maria Theresa, the fenced-in yards had been filled in with sheds, goat pens, rabbit hutches, and privies. Somewhere in the middle there was a well, often boarded up, with pump and pump handle, just a few feet from the privy with its cesspool. Sometimes there would be a few square meters of sparse grass, a few sickly bushes, and even a fruit tree—so few trees that one could count them easily. The inhabitants of a house possessing such a tree would count the apples and pears before they ripened and guarded them day and night. The results of all of this clutter were rotting backyards, contaminated with stinking putrefaction. Almost all the wells were contaminated, their water a slimy green color. Quick action was necessary. Thus began the renovation.

In the blocks all the fences were removed, the contaminated wells were filled or their pumps removed. All pens and sheds were torn down. The privies in the yards were closed, the cesspools filled in, and sanitary cess-

Inner court.
(Courtesy Leo Baeck Institute)

pools were constructed, made of concrete and topped with primitive but sanitary latrines. Wherever possible, indoor privies with connections to the cesspools were constructed. In front of every closed privy—one for a two-story house—there would be a rough-hewn wooden table with a tin washbasin on it containing a mixture of water and chlorine, with an elderly male or female ghetto resident sitting next to it as the privy guard. Every occupant—after leaving—would be reminded by the guard: "Please wash your hands." The old folks {doing this service} would get an increase in their bread ration, which they badly needed.

Little courtyard.
(Courtesy Leo Baeck Institute)

The German nationals {doing} privy guard were especially remarkable. No "please" for them; they took their office very seriously. They would wear a leather or cloth belt with a crossbelt over the shoulders, and they wore a visored cap. There they would stand, serious and taciturn; duty is duty, no room for jokes. "Would you be good enough to wash your hands?" Ah yes, the Germans, we Germans, have discipline.

After all the trash and odds and ends were removed from the court-yards, a spacious, easily manageable yard would remain that could be cleaned without trouble. A few simply fashioned benches and tables could be set up, and there was room to breathe. The department of pest control closed one house after the other and fumigated them thoroughly. Thus we got rid of lice, fleas, and bedbugs. This sanitation process in the contaminated garrison town took a few months. The barracks were rela-tively clean and so was the hospital in the Hohenelbe barracks as well as the smaller sickrooms distributed among the civilian dwellings.

The general supervision of the ghetto was strictly regulated. In spite of that a typhus epidemic erupted during my stay, which prompted des-perate efforts to stop it. There were many deaths, the hospitals were crowded, but the danger was shortly brought under control. . . .[5]

I seem to remember that I arrived in the ghetto in March or April 1942. Everything was still in the beginning stages, and a start was made at orga-nization and creation of order out of the chaos of the transports.

In Theresienstadt we had not yet become the anonymous numbers we later became in Auschwitz. We still had our names, though we had to take on a new collective name: all men were called "Israel" as part of their first name and all women were "Sara."[6]

We also had to get used to other peculiarities: we invisible persons of the ghetto had to submit to an unaccustomed social order. In our pre-vious lives, our civilian lives, we used to work to pay for {our} housing, nutrition, clothing, education, public service, taxes, etc., out of our income. In the Ghetto Theresienstadt this arrangement changed radically. We formed a society that had to function without money. No one of us received the customary Friday pay envelope. But on the main square a bank was set up. The director of the bank was the Viennese head of the Jewish Community, a very respected man.[7]

Books were kept assiduously in the bank, keeping track of fictitious salaries of every working ghetto inmate, which, however, were never paid to anyone. Every inmate really did have an account in his name at the bank. Whether he was transported East later on was immaterial.

Here I have to mention a striking irony. After the end of World War II and the destruction of Hitler's Third Reich, the Czech authorities who took over Theresienstadt including the bank did pay out to the survivors who had been deported from Theresienstadt and returned from the East their accumulated monies in their name. They paid them in Czech crowns. I do not remember at what exchange value they paid them.[8]

For us ghetto inmates, this new social order did indeed represent a readjustment. We existed, we worked in certain labor categories, either more or less close to the profession we had previously held or any place we had been assigned to.

We patiently lined up for coffee in the morning, soup or a potato at noon, most of the time turnips or some such inedible stuff, and evenings for coffee and lentil pod soup. With that we got approximately one-half a loaf of bread—our only true sustenance—per day. We were forever hungry, and most of us lost forty to fifty pounds within three weeks in the ghetto.

Everyone was assigned quarters. They consisted of a straw mattress (filled with excelsior) and a pillow, two blankets spread on the floor, or a bedstead in the barracks or an attic or in any kind of crowded room in the dirty civilian houses available. Only the members of the Council of Elders, prominente, and the Danes had separate rooms for themselves and their wives.

{Only} the most basic necessities of daily life were provided. "We had nothing, but that we had for sure." We lived from day to day—a totally new concept—one could {almost} say without care if we hadn't been filled constantly with worries. They were a drain on the nerves, on the strongest resistance. Who, after all, can get used to {the idea of} eventually having to face the transports and to suspect that there {would be} no way back from there? No death sentence has been rendered, no court has condemned us, we are all innocent—except for being Jews—but we cannot escape. Is no one supposed to get stomach ulcers this way? And no, hardly anyone ever got them. The general health of the young people was good, perhaps just because they were so starved. But if they fell ill with a virus, pneumonia, typhus, etc., then the afflicted persons had no resistance whatsoever and died like flies.

9

LOVE AND SEX IN THERESIENSTADT

If a marriage were a bit wobbly, as was frequently the case in some of the small towns where the couple only remained together because of the children and because of "what people would say," then all such scruples disappeared shortly in the ghetto without the slightest consideration {for appearances}. Of course, if there were children, the family would meet for supper, but immediately after that, each went his own way: the wife to her lover—frequently someone else's husband—the husband to his mistress.

The restraints, controlled until now, disappeared, {giving way to} the simple, primitive, desperate desire, the irresistible urge, the compulsion to share the few hours that life might still allow; to share the grace, the felicity of love with the person who means everything. Who could condemn any one of these; who could condemn the last blessed hours of love? Any day the next transport could bury forever these passionate ecstasies, could end a great love suddenly, could bury the lovers forever.

Many Brünn love affairs within the so-called better circles that had been wrapped in secrecy until now, only known to the participants, came to light here: openly, uninhibited, without the slightest restraint. Until now the affairs had been conducted out of town, in Vienna, abroad, or in winter sport resorts, but now there was hardly any opposition from the respective partners. Restraints, morals, ethical considerations? What morals? What rules of ethics? Yes, how love complicated everything; every second must be lived to its fullest. Not one moment of love must remain unfulfilled—until the eastern transport does us part. No life filled with love is waiting for us. Hours, days, sometimes weeks, perhaps, of indescribable happiness. Then comes the notice, personally delivered, {bringing} shock, horrified desperation: "assigned to the next transport."

Everyone packs; two days later the train leaves for an unknown destination—unknown to the passengers—to the East toward extermination. Inhibitions disappeared; ethics, morals were forgotten. What remained was the tragic, doomed love, lived with the highest intensity.

The question of course arises that so much love, such intense love, must inevitably lead to the active act of love, to sex. Was there a sex life in the ghetto, in the concentration camps? Here I must qualify my answer: only in the Ghetto Theresienstadt. And how white-hot, how determined it was, in spite of the many obstacles and difficulties.

In Theresienstadt, the ghetto, there were numerically as many men as there were women, of all ages, tightly crowded together, but separated in barracks under primitive living conditions, starving, working hard, living on borrowed time. They were relatively unguarded but not free, {although they} did not have to worry about the basic necessities and thus the idea of sex could not be far off. Only a very few had the privilege of living and sleeping in seclusion together. The rest of us found ways and means to enjoy, however fleetingly, the blissful intimacy between lovers that we shall call sex. . . .

In spite of the fact that a Nazi concentration camp has a similar function as a prison, it is hardly possible to compare the two. Prisons are solid, fortresslike buildings in which criminals are locked away and separated from society at large for shorter or longer periods. They are under the jurisdiction of a strict system, the sexes are kept separate, and housing as well as food is sufficiently provided for. In these surroundings sex is possible; however, only the homosexual kind.

Concentration camps, on the other hand, are almost exclusively provided for people of both sexes who are not criminals because they are opponents, critics of the regime in question. The Nazis had designated as enemies of the state all Jews, Gypsies, and all minorities and nations who refused to "be restored to spiritual health through the Germanic essence," and other similar slogans.

The concentration camps that had been newly created in all of occupied Europe were not the permanent kind. They were camps with widely spaced barracks . . . surrounded by electrically charged barbed-wire fences, two to three meters high, with guard towers at regular intervals and an entrance gate with a toll-bar. The entrance gate was sometimes decorated with a wooden framework, but more often these frameworks were made of iron and always featured the cynically idiotic inscription: "*arbeit macht frei*" {"work liberates"}.

The system displayed an unbearably sadistic cruelty. The wooden or brick barracks with their two- or three-story bedsteads, insufficient heating, and few washing facilities could only be compared to cattle sheds.

Corporal punishment, flogging, torture, extremely heavy manual labor assured a prisoner that his chances of survival were minimal.

A concentration camp was no place for sex. If any of these emaciated
skeletons with their pale, shrunken skin, without flesh, without muscles,
wrapped in their striped rags, would look at one another, any thought of a
not-so-distant past when they were still strong, well-nourished men, for
whom women meant love and sex, would vanish from their minds. However, if there were women somewhere near, even if they were completely
separated from us, as for instance in Auschwitz, the same old story of love
without sex would start again, in a different form, sublimated, distant, but
all the more intense.

Not any one of the new arrivals to the ghetto, insecure, waiting to be
assigned to the next or any future transport, was in the mood to even
think of sex, but love was important. Surviving was the main goal, to
remain in Theresienstadt.

At that time Theresienstadt meant for us, together with thousands of
our brothers and sisters, a kind of impermanent shelter. . . . True, it was
incomparably worse than our home, but nevertheless we were at least in
our home country, which was incomparably better than the unknown
East, the mere thought of which filled every one of us with unspeakable
horrors, with paralyzing fear. In this state of mind love is the only refuge.
Utter despair and life-threatening anxieties are better borne when there
are two {people}.

In these first months I was—divorced—alone and lonesome. I was despondent in having witnessed the disappearance of Alice, Dora, and Sari
to the East. I buried myself in work at the architectural office during this
unhappy time and worked on cleaning the town that was overrun by
vermin and on improving the latrines. I was satisfied to share my drafting
room with my colleagues, to talk shop, and to stand in line at the food
distribution place—anything to put off the inevitable return to my quar-

ters that I shared with a few hundred other men of every kind and age, of the most diverse intellectual backgrounds.

There was no woman, no girlfriend with whom I could share my worries, with whom I could forget my despair. The little parks in the town were always filled with thousands of people. Outside of town, outside of the walls, the lovely pastoral, calming, eternal, Bohemian landscape called to me, the landscape that I later sketched and painted, so often motivated by pure escapism. On top of that, men and women were strictly separated. Imagine a barracks with 3,000–4,000 tightly crowded women with the hundreds of babies belonging to them.

As life slowly stabilized, there developed in Theresienstadt a kind of society comprising several levels:

1. The upper level—not exactly aristocracy—those who were unconditionally protected from transports, or so it seemed: the Council of Elders, the AK1 and AK2.

2. The officialdom of workers who were absolutely indispensable for the functioning of the ghetto: waterworks, power station, hospital, sewage, the smithy, agriculture, and their "spongers." The drafting department, the technical department, altogether approximately 10,000 men,[1] protected from transport, together with one to four members of their families.

3. The children and the old people. We tried every which way to keep the children until peace would finally arrive, but we did not succeed. Like their parents, the children were finally also sent east where almost all of them died.[2] The old people, critically undernourished, died like flies of gastroenteritis and decrepitude and starved by the hundreds.

4. The newly arrived unprotected transports, which sooner or later would be filling the eastbound transports.

I belonged to the second category. I felt, I hoped and knew by experience, that I was protected from the transports. This feeling of relative security almost automatically gave rise to my interest in women, in love, and in sex. But this reawakened interest had to take second place to start with, because there were many obstacles that repressed any feelings of love.

Like everyone else I suffered greatly from hunger, so that I was plagued all through the day with thoughts of the kind of food I had been used to, as compared to the food we received, the daily turnip soup menu with an unpeeled potato and the half loaf of bread. Until that time I {had} hardly ever suffered the pangs of hunger—I could fast for one day during Yom Kippur—but here, without any transition, our rations were shortened to such an extent (approximately one-third of the customary calories in their most unappetizing form) that hunger weakened and absorbed {one's} every thought. In a four-week period I lost twenty-five kilos.

It took three to four months until one reached a plateau where the pangs of hunger—real pains that reduced one's thinking and working abilities—were less apparent, because it seems that the human organism can get used to hunger as well. This intense feeling, the extreme urge to provide more food to the emaciated body, led inevitably to everyone's attempt to buy, that is, trade for, food according to the individual ability and skill, mainly the ability to have access to smuggled-in cigarettes. Smokers, hooked on cigarettes, on the other hand, rather would suffer from hunger than give up their cigarettes.

In my free time I made several contacts with fellow prisoners who directly or indirectly were connected with food in every form: cooks, bakers, but especially "capitalists" who would regularly receive supplies of food from the hinterland. The sketches that I saved amply document the source of my food supply. How many of the sketches and watercolors that probably were worth a lot more did I trade in the bakery or in one of the many kitchens: a good drawing for a loaf of bread, a watercolor for one and a half loaves of bread or two yeast dumplings and three big potatoes.

Not everyone was a patron of the arts; thus I was left with many sketches. It would take approximately two hours' work to sketch the dough machines in the bakery or the soup kettles and wooden vats in the kitchens, but {the sketches} would be bought for double portions of soup or two yeast dumplings or three to four potatoes. I would also paint the lodgings of the cooks who had quarters in the dark, underground casemates. I would paint southern Mediterranean landscapes on the whitewashed vaults, which would create the illusion of being in Portofino or in Capri instead of the reality of the dank dungeons sparsely lit by barred windows.

With the help of this itinerant artwork I slowly managed to overcome the eternally torturing, nagging hunger. Monumental hunger creates indifference toward all other emotions such as love and sex. An eternally growling stomach drowns out whisperings of love, need of sleep, fatigue, angst. Indifference makes one immune to sex. This immunity was increased by the unbearable housing conditions. How can one arrange a tête-à-tête in a room one shares with 100–300 men, or on the lawn or one of the few park benches, crammed together like on Jones Beach even though one begins to put out feelers to find female companions, someone to talk with, to share one's thoughts and cares with? And in the background always the worry, the fear: What if she is assigned to a transport and I cannot protect her? How often did I have to watch one of these dear, intimate creatures disappear into an eastbound transport. The poor heart dies slowly, torn by too many wounds inflicted by the eternal good-byes. But slowly even the heart becomes accustomed to facing continual pain with composure; until the day one is fortunate enough to find someone who is also protected.

We make a date in front of the church at 6:00 P.M. after the food distribution. How do I find her in the crowd as dense as at St. Patrick's on Easter Sunday? But finally I have her hand in mine. Where shall we go? To which café, which movie?[3] We find a bench somewhere to sit down. This is no place for intimacy, masses of people around us, like Times Square. Nevertheless, we attempt to continue our lovers' conversation in snatches. My kingdom for the smallest room, a cubbyhole, a kumbal. This was only granted to me at a later date.

Thus after my six months in the ghetto, and with a shrunken stomach, I was pretty well protected from transports. {My} love interest was protected as well, but {we had} no privacy, only the mere appearance of it. But then our department head, Era Kohn, succeeded in arranging for special quarters for the twelve members of my group in the technical department. We moved from the overcrowded quarters in the Sudeten barracks to a fairly large room in the Hannover barracks. We fixed it up comfortably.

To provide enough room in the center for a simple table with benches that were roughly nailed together we built double bunks along the walls; the upper bunks were the better ones because you did not hit your head every time you got up. We drew lots for the upper bunks. In spite of the close quarters, we were happy at least to have escaped the overcrowding. And "privacy" began. . . .

Each bed, or rather, each "couch," was enclosed on three sides instead of being open on all sides as before. Along the wall, the two ugly headboards served as shelving; one side would be closed off with a sheet or blanket. It was open to the front. Later, just as in a sleeping car, there would be a dyed sheet on a wire to close the front. The whole thing was a sort of poster bed. The setting for the start of a not exactly active love life was in place.

Our imagination conjured up wild, erotic dreams in fantastic colors of pink and violet. Like our yeast dumplings, they collapsed in the cool air of reality. A wild love life, embraces inside a two-meter by seventy-five

centimeter–sized box made out of sheets with eleven listeners and witnesses? Our fantasy-inspired dreams of love ended in sober awakening.

Something had to be done. The room commandant, a perfect gentleman, Ing. Baron, and three of the married roommates called a meeting to
decide what to do to give everyone at least the appearance, at least a
minimum, of privacy. Only by the consensus of all twelve roommates
could we arrive at a solution, a referendum with a two-thirds majority.
We all knew that two of our colleagues would be principally opposed to
such a solution: Roubiček, the red-headed "ugly dwarf," a surveyor, who
was simply antisocial by nature, had no friends, and could find no girlfriend. The other one, an Ing. Rosenbaum, used to be normal, but under
the continual pressure he had turned into a grouch and a religious fanatic.
During the time between work and sleep he wrapped himself into a *tallith*
{prayer shawl}, covered his head, prayed in a singsong melody, bowing
continually in the orthodox manner. We could understand why he re-
treated into religious belief, but the *schammes* {the Jewish equivalent of a
beadle}, as we called him, prayed in German because he did not know a
word of Hebrew. There were a lot of *meshuggenah* {crazy people} in the
ghetto who were not locked away in our *cvokárna* {"nuthouse" in Czech
slang}, our improvised insane asylum.

After lengthy consideration it was unanimously—minus two—decided
to institute an unalterable schedule, that is, on certain days at the express
wish of the parties concerned, the locked room would be off limits to
everyone for two hours at a time. When it was Roubiček's turn, since he
had no girl, he had to wait grimly until the door was unlocked. Rosenbaum had a wife, but since he spent his free time praying, she had found
herself another young admirer. When {Rosenbaum's} turn came, he would
pray, locked in by himself, with doubled intensity, at one with his God.

The schedule we had set up worked very well as long as it did not conflict with the schedule of the loved ones, the wives or girlfriends. You could not exchange your place in the schedule. If you did not use it, it lapsed.

We lived in this "engineers' room" for a year. We got used to each other, we knew about our former lives, each other's thoughts, each other's weaknesses, and especially about ourselves. You simply cannot scream in agony when colleague Glaser would start for the twelfth time to recount his adventures on his trip to Venice in detail. If we were in a good mood, and he began {to relate the story of his journey to} Venice, for instance . . . , we would repeat the whole story back to him in chorus. Ing. Baron with his tenor voice could sing whole phrases and melodies from Mozart's Marriage of Figaro, which we enjoyed hugely. Some other nights, so I would not feel left out, the chorus would chime in on my old story of how I spent the night with an old flame named Sophie only half unwillingly in Franzensberg Park. (The park in question in Brünn had a gate that would close at 9:00 P.M. in summer and 7:00 P.M. in winter.)

I was well acquainted with a problem that was prevalent among even very sophisticated prisoners; that is, after a relatively short time you ran out of topics of conversation. I experienced it as a young officer in World War I. In spite of the interval of twenty years in which I had accumulated (supposedly) a large amount of experiences and had read hundreds of books and completed five years of university studies, in spite of a good memory, there comes a time when one begins to repeat oneself. You lose the spontaneity, the sense of humor; however, you do not lose the need for conversation, to be amused, to see others laugh, to impress others with how intelligent, worldly, wise, and humorous you are. Without new stimuli, without new experiences, new books, the day arrives when you feel that sterility has set in, like impotence; it is a traumatic shock.

The period of bearable coexistence with professional colleagues suddenly ended for me, temporarily at least. My love interest, like me, safe from transports, Hanička, a petite brunette with big eyes and blue-black hair, really very beautiful, was in the ghetto with two sons, eight and ten. Her husband was in England and had been trying unsuccessfully to smuggle her out of Czechoslovakia. In the meantime she had had several love affairs, and as she had hesitated too long to leave, she had finally landed in Theresienstadt. She was working in the hospital where I met her when I spent a few weeks there after an operation. It was our bad luck that her free time did not coincide with mine. I had Thursdays from 4:00–6:00 reserved in our schedule. She was off every day between 2:00 and 4:00. Therefore I could not meet her in our twelve-man room on Thursdays between 4:00 and 6:00. What cursed luck! But she had a girlfriend in the commissary who had been clever enough to have found a kumbal, a little cubbyhole under a staircase in the cellar of a civilian dwelling, and to arrange it so skillfully that it resembled a tiny *pied-à-terre* without a bathroom. The girlfriend let Hanička use the kumbal from 2:00 to 4:00.

Taking a considerable risk, I got off from work on that day between 2:00 and 4:00. Excited, full of anticipation, bursting with happiness, carrying a sheaf of files under my arm so as not to attract any attention, I hurried to our rendezvous. It was a lovely summer day, blue skies, the houses along one side of the street threw deep shadows onto the other side. Only a few people were about; it was working time until 6:00. I was in a good mood, active, full of life, what you would call "healthy."

All of a sudden, without any prior warning, without any reason, really like a bolt out of the blue, my knees buckled. Within seconds I felt kind of faint, an overwhelming weakness, a hot flush across my forehead. I had only one desire, to lie down and sleep. I could just barely drag myself to the gate where we were to meet and where I had to sit down on the doorstep, enfeebled. Hanička arrived at the same time. She saw immediately that I was in critical condition, took my arm, and led me back to the entrance of my barracks and arranged right afterward for a litter with two bearers who took me to the nearest sickroom, one of the small satellite hospitals, in a private house where I lost consciousness.

When I awoke I was in a cast-iron bed with a mattress, like in a {real} hospital, and the head physician was bending over me and checking whether or not my heart was beating. The head physician was Dr. Helena Gutmann, an incredibly able and very humane physician from Prague. In spite of the fact that I was not quite conscious, and still delirious, I could not help noticing that the doctor was a beauty, reddish-blond and well built. Who could have known that at a later date I would almost marry her? At the time she was married to one of the best physicians of Prague. How absurd life can be; how totally beyond our control.

At that time in that little hospital I was really seriously ill. I had a severe case of pneumonia, a disease that was extremely dangerous for us in the ghetto because of our weakened, undernourished constitutions and mainly because of the desperate lack of medical supplies. I found out much later that Dr. Gutmann arranged, at great risk to herself, to get the sulfonamide pills, newly on the market at that time, which she prescribed for me. I overcame the crisis of the disease and began to recuperate slowly. I have absolutely no doubt that I owe my life to the beautiful head physician and her ceaseless devotion and care, day and night, that summer of 1943. Because of her care I did not succumb to pneumonia. The good Lord above and my watchful guardian angel Gabriel as well as the affection of my physician, at the time still unknown to me—all that contributed in considerable measure toward my recuperation.

Dr. Gutmann survived the war but lost her husband during its last days. She was very successful in her career, and I have heard that she is at present working in a hospital in West Germany. My subsequent reunion with her in Prague after the war belongs to another chapter of my life.

After my release from the hospital I returned to my former quarters with my eleven roommates in the Hannover barracks. Everything was as

"Bubi" Windholz.
(Courtesy Leo Baeck Institute)

before, but I was emaciated and weakened. My neighbor on the next bed was architect Windholz, {affectionately} called "Bubi." He was my friend, and I liked him very much. He was reliable, decent, steady, imperturbable. He was a "Bubi," delicate but wiry, a little black Chaplin mustache under a slightly crooked boxer's nose with a thick head of black hair. His wife was the exact opposite: thick-set, a bit hefty, strong, always in a good mood. She would come daily to visit her "Bubi" in our room and cooked the evening meal for the two of them, prepared artfully on the communal electric hot plate that we kept secretly, like everybody else in Theresienstadt who could get hold of one. After my return from the hospital they looked after me and helped me slowly to overcome my weakened condition. Throughout my stay in the ghetto they remained dear and close friends.

The complete lack of vitamins, fresh vegetables, or fruit of course contributed greatly to the weakened condition of nearly all ghetto inhabitants, especially the convalescent. The women were ingenious enough to create soups and salads out of all kinds of herbs and grasses such as dandelion and ribwort {a weed}. In an emergency the Jew will eat grass.[4]

10

A TASTE OF FREEDOM

One day I received an unusual and unexpected commission from the Council of Elders, according to a memorandum from {Nazi} headquarters, to design for {the SS} a large coat of arms—in color—of the city. This commission was followed shortly after by another one, a bird's-eye view of Theresienstadt and the surrounding area, two and a half meters long and one and a quarter meters high. This commission brought an unexpected bonus. Upon my request I was issued a pass that allowed me to leave the ghetto, to roam freely within an area of three kilometers to do the necessary sketching.

I had hit the jackpot. How could I have painted a detailed bird's-eye view of Theresienstadt if only seeing the town from the inside? The client insisted on details. Thus I began my daily excursions into the surrounding area outside of the fortress. I sketched every house, every tree, the fortifications, the moats, the ramparts, and then the surrounding landscape. What a great spiritual and mental uplift {for me}!

The landscape of this part of Bohemia is especially lovely, unspoiled and undisturbed by industrial landmarks like telegraph poles, factory chimneys, a crematorium, and the like. The meadows were of a brilliant green, crisscrossed by country lanes, separated by clumps of bushes where pheasants and partridges would fly up when disturbed, an occasional curious hare sitting in the shade of a tree. So quiet and solemn, a bohemian Arcadia, a comforting, unending loveliness. In the distance a single peak, Mt. Řip, on the other side a fertile valley, a steeple surrounded by red roofs, the town of Leitmeritz {Litoměřice} surrounded by mountains shimmering in the blue haze. How was I to know how much I would curse this town and the orchard-covered mountainsides?

I continued to produce my sketches. The outside of the Fortress Theresienstadt did not look threatening at all; it looked almost like a park. From the outside you did not see anything of the twelve to fifteen meter–high brick walls of the fortification. All the roofs of the complicated defense installations were covered with dirt to heights of two meters and featured luxuriant, well-tended lawns, even some stands of trees. The fortifications on the periphery ran out into grass-covered slopes at the level of the plain. Dense stands of trees made it appear like a park. Even the gates of the fortress did not look threatening.

Through one of the gates the road led directly across the bridge over

Town of Leitmeritz.
(*Courtesy Leo Baeck Institute*)

the Eger River to the gate of the feared and accursed Little Fortress that everyone tried to avoid like the plague. At the end of a long lane of what I believe were linden trees, you could see a dark red brick wall with a gate painted in a black-and-white alternating pattern, which seemed to give the gate its dangerous, threatening, and forbidding appearance. At that time I did not know yet that that gate would close behind me one day, and I would pass {back} through it barely alive.

The Eger River flowed between the gates of the Ghetto Theresienstadt and the Little Fortress, a satellite fort. The bridge connecting the two sides of the road was at the same time a dam for a power plant, serving the adjacent sluice mill, an old mill {decorated} with some baroque ornamen-

Ramparts.
(Courtesy Leo Baeck Institute)

tation. The bright green house of the mill owner faced the mill. That group of structures, the mill, the green house, the bridge, became my favorite motif, which I used to sketch over and over in any kind of light.

Within the allowed perimeter of three kilometers I pretty soon knew every tree, every shed, every stable, and especially the orchards. There was no one to be seen, and if an SS guard would pass, I would sit innocently and paint. They would stop, startled to see a Jew with a star running around free and painting. I would show my pass, and they would leave me alone. At that time the orchards were full of the most wonderful apples and pears to be had for the taking. One reach and I had filled myself with vitamins. In that period athletes like me would wear the fashionable knickerbockers, which would fall loosely over the knee and were buckled

Mill.
(Courtesy Leo Baeck Institute)

below it. I wore a pair of corduroy ones, {which served as} two bags tied around my legs that I would fill carefully with about six to ten apples or pears. No one noticed it, and thus I could have my sister Ida and my colleagues, protectors, and friends share in my wealth. Fruit was also a good trading item for bread. . . .

During my expeditions into the immediate vicinity of the Ghetto Theresienstadt I had discovered a little house with a gable roof painted the K and K yellow {*Kaiser-und-Königliches gelb*, "imperial" color for official residences of the Austro-Hungarian Empire}. It was situated on a lonely side road near the Little Fortress on a wonderfully romantic lawn, shaded by leafy oaks and maples. Around the house stood carts and hay wagons that are commonly used by farmers.

The scene was so idyllic and pastoral that I immediately sat down on the closest tree stump and began to sketch it. While sketching I heard the typical noises of a smithy coming out of the one-story house through the wide door, the hammer hitting the hot iron on the anvil. After a while a powerfully built man, slightly sooty and wearing a leather apron, stepped out of the house and went to one of the carts whose axle he was repairing. He saw me, came closer, looked at the sketch that showed his smithy and hay wagon; he continued fidgeting with the cart and asked me under his breath what I was doing, whether I came from Terezín, whether I was hungry, all this in Czech.

I had to answer yes to his last question, and I explained my activity to him. He avoided standing next to me and talking directly to me. He puttered around and talked sotto voce into the air. Then he returned to the smithy, saying one word in Czech: "čekej" ("wait"). Later he came out again, worked around the hay wagon, and dropped a small package with the words "dej pozor" ("be careful"). "Come again tomorrow." With that he disappeared. I bent down unobtrusively and hid the package in my knickerbockers. Upon opening it in our quarters I found it to contain two thick slices of bread, thickly spread with lard and pork cracklings, a princely dish that lasted me for two to three days. From that time on I met the smith, whose name I have forgotten, practically daily. I never stepped inside the smithy. I had to be very careful to be able to notice unwanted intruders easily without being seen myself. There was always a package ready for me, sometimes with buchteln, sometimes with kolatschen {Czech yeast-dough pastries} filled with prune preserves.

Those were good times, and he was a good man; for my depressed, hopeless spirit this simple, kindhearted smith represented the small flick-

Smithy.
(Courtesy Leo Baeck Institute)

ering light of hope. An unknown from the outside world, not a Nazi, someone who out of the goodness of his heart did not chase the poor Jew with his yellow star, despised by all the world, from his doorstep. He exposed himself to considerable danger if he would have been seen with me. He took a calculated risk to help a condemned fellow human being, a Jew. I fervently hope that the heavens saw the good deeds of the smith and will have rewarded him.

After the war, when I visited Theresienstadt as a survivor, I found the smithy still in its idyllic location. But no carts; the smithy was deserted; no sign of life; the roof was damaged, the few window panes broken. How easily such a deserted, decayed smithy can destroy an idyll, a romantic memory.

I must also add that the owner of the sluice mill that I painted so often gave me some bread in exchange for a few paintings. After I had delivered the big bird's-eye view, my excursions into "freedom" literally came to an end. No more vitamins, only the hunger remained.

This fortunate episode of being able to paint on an official commission outside of our prison-ghetto, an undreamed-of privilege, only lasted six weeks. To be able to steal fruit and to receive gifts from the good blacksmith were added benefits. From then on I worked again in the drafting room, "designed" primitive toilets, called latrines, and from time to time also a new barracks building that was needed. I used my free time now to sketch as quickly as possible everything around me in the ghetto.

I assumed imprudently that the captivity would end one day, and I collected as complete a record as possible of my present life for comparisons at a later date; if ever I would feel I was too well off, I would be reminded of the past.

In spite of the eternal insecurity of life—as regards the transports to the East—I lived for the day and counted on surviving the inevitable end of the Third Reich because of my protection from transports. But, as Bertolt Brecht said: "Circumstances are not like that." As interest in exchanging my sketches for bread and soup waned but my hunger remained, I began to look around for other sources of supply.

11

"KUMBALISTICS"

I will discuss this episode under the title, "Kumbalistics," a {word from} Czech ghetto slang. A kumbal in Czech is an attic or a small cubbyhole so "kumbalistika" could be translated into "attic architecture."

The privileged, permanently protected inmates, such as the Council of Elders and the groups known as AK1 and AK2, were intent on expanding their privileges to {include} private quarters away from the overcrowded ones. Inside and outside of the barracks, but especially in the former housing of the civilian population, one could find corners, cubbyholes, spaces under the staircases.

The bakers especially had a surplus of nooks and crannies, as the bakery from its beginning had been built into the fortification. Everywhere in the barracks there were pantries, cellars, and casematelike vaults that could be transformed into comfortable kumbals with a bit of imagination, a lot of stolen lumber, and a few sheets, dyed blue. I knew a group of cooks in the kitchen of the Dresdner barracks where my "unprotected" sister-in-law worked as well. In two recesses of a fairly large cubicle they had placed their straw sacks on the floor and had built a few wooden shelves along the walls.

Once, when we were in the process of exchanging one of my kitchen sketches for two yeast dumplings, I mentioned that I could make a very comfortable kumbal out of their two recesses, and I quickly sketched a design to show them. They were delighted, and we started to discuss the details such as how many sheets were needed, how many boards, nails, etc. The honorarium: one {loaf of} bread or ten cigarettes per occupant. I was in business. In Theresienstadt such activities became part of the gossip, and with this commission began my stomach-filling career of "kumbalistics."

Soon I was called on by the bakers, the wealthiest capitalists, who were able to hoard the "gold" (read bread). Of course the head of the bakery and his assistants belonged to the ghetto aristocracy, AK1: privileged. They could well afford to invite people to supper, having access to flour, margarine, sugar, etc., and they also could afford to make contact with the hinterland, via the gendarmes. I succeeded in creating for the head of the bakery a really nice, practical apartment (two rooms). This apartment was seen by one of the visitors to the bakers, Ing. Gruenberger, a member of the Council of Elders and my department head as well as my protector.

Council of Elders members had been assigned one vaulted room each in the Magdeburger barracks where they were allowed to live with their wives; however, without the least bit of luxury. {Their quarters} were primitive and simple. Ing. Gruenberger was impressed enough to invite me a few days later to his "house," asking me what I could make out of his room. {Troller had already decorated Ing. Zucker's quarters.} He and his charming wife presented their ideas to me, and after a few days, when they had seen my plans and the color sketches for the room, we started to work and within four days they hardly recognized their room; it had become an apartment. Dr. Murmelstein engaged me also shortly thereafter, and I became persona grata in the inner circle of the establishment of the Council of Elders. They of course did not have to steal the materials; they could requisition them from the lumberyard.

This contact was of great importance to me. It gave me access to the innermost circle in those critical days when transports were being arranged The members of the council would sit in seclusion, locked in, with the fearsome task of selecting 1,000 or more innocent victims, to assign their brethren to transports to the East, which they knew only too well would lead to their deaths. Desperate struggles took place behind the scenes to save some individuals, until the next transport at least. . . .

I have no difficulty in documenting my activity as a kumbal architect, since I managed to save approximately a dozen or so of the working drawings and colored perspectives together with my other sketches. How my reputation as architect ever reached the SS headquarters has remained a puzzle to me. This has nothing to do with that bird's-eye view.

Sometime in 1943 I received a memorandum, a formal request, to design a museum in the headquarters. Among my sketches there were two colored designs for the project. What I did not know at the time was that the main purpose of this was to produce professionally and artistically rendered charts and exhibits so that the Red Cross Commission could be impressed, that is, duped; have the wool pulled over their eyes.[1]

Kumbals.
(Courtesy Leo Baeck Institute)

A few weeks later, a new memo appeared, marked "Ing. Troller," directing me to appear at the SS quarters (kameradschaftsheim) to design a tap room, dining room, and large lobby with fireplace. This "commission" was a great shock to me. Everyone in the ghetto did his best to avoid any contact with the SS; it was preferable to remain anonymous. If they like what you do, your pay is a kick or {the "compliment"} "pig of a Jew" but under no circumstances a loaf of bread or a cigarette. If they do not like it, it could mean the immense risk of being assigned to the next transport.

All my attempts to dodge the commission were in vain. The SS quarters was the only fairly modern hotel in Theresienstadt, which was used as a domicile for the SS. The public rooms were old-fashioned and shabby. I think it must have been Dr. Seidl,[2] the SS camp commander, who barked at the mute Norbert "Israel" Troller, giving various orders and directives that only genuine German elements of style could be used for the designs. He requested to see sample designs in color. Frescoes were to express a military theme.

When I had finished the colored sketches as well as the plans and the detailed drawings, I reported to the technical department, and the Council of Elders informed the commander at the daily briefing. Two days later another memo: Ing. Norbert Israel Troller to appear on such and such a day at 3:00 P.M. in the SS quarters. I appeared there on time. Enter Seidl with the sketches and with him Obersturmführer {First Lieutenant} Burger, whom everyone coming from Brünn knew and feared.[3] He was a fanatic, a cruel, brutal sadist, who had organized the transports from Brünn. He detested Jews so vehemently that any time he was in the offices of the Jewish Community, he would open the doors only with his elbow, so that he would not dirty his hands with "Jewish emanations." He was a gigantic and terrifying imbecile. He was holding my perspective of the lobby with the fireplace.

On both sides of the fireplace I had sketched a tall candelabra, as in a

Troller's sketch of the SS mess hall with "Jewish" candelabra crossed out.
(Courtesy Leo Baeck Institute)

church. Both had been marked out with an X. His forefinger on the X, he yelled at me: "No Jew candelabras in this hall, you Jewish pig!" and slapped me twice in the face. Nevertheless, the rooms were executed exactly to my design—without the "Jew candelabras." Somehow the designs were saved as well with the rest of my sketches. The military wall paintings were the design of my friend, the well-known Dutch painter Jo Spier.[4]

12

THE ETERNAL ROMANTIC

One thing we all had in common: the heartrending and tragic awareness of the impermanence of human relationships, the underlying fear of a permanent commitment. How can the wonderful feeling of loving and being loved, without a care, ever grow when one is aware of the eternally torturing question: how long, when will the transports separate us?

Thus relationships developed that were inevitably ambiguous. On the one hand, there was spontaneous, true, eternal love; on the other, we were faced with the continual threat of separation, sex, lust, a pressure cooker atmosphere, quick, quick, without fancy phrases, before the next transport to the East stops us, because no one returned from there. Only to find a space, a kumbal, a cellar, an attic, where two people could be alone, to "sleep together" for an hour. Next day they would disappear into the crowd. If they did know each other's name, they soon forgot it.

Of course there were some permanent arrangements for the limited number of privileged ones of AK1 and AK2, for the so-called prominenten so designated by the SS, "some few" distinguished former citizens of the German Reich, and the Danes, who were under special protection and who survived the war and the end of the Third Reich in Theresienstadt.[1] All the other privileged ones finally also ended up in the transports late in 1944.[2]

The separation of young and not so young lovers was heartbreaking to watch until the habit of seeing this, even for the compassionate heart, dulled compassion and throttled it. It can be compared to the frightful shock of seeing death for the first time if in a hospital the man in the bed next to you dies. After having watched a dozen or so die next to you, death does not make an impression anymore.

My own experience can give a more concrete picture of the relationships in our crowded prison situation. At the time I was a healthy, skinny man in my prime, filled with passion, romanticism, and a lively imagination. My hunger for life, love, and sex was great. The fact that I lacked a private space, some intimate quarters, prevented the satisfaction of these appetites. But the situation changed in 1943.

We, the deserving veterans, the principal coworkers of Era Kohn's group, we twelve roommates from the Hannover barracks received permission, the privilege, to build individual kumbals in the attic of the house #3-E11b, which contained a small bakery. The kumbals were not to exceed six by eight square meters. We started work feverishly; nights we went to the lumberyard to steal wood scraps. My cousin, the manager of the lumberyard, made me a present of a few nice, long boards with knot-holes. In the *kleiderkammer* {clothing depot} where thousands of "ge-schleuste" {"stolen"} blankets were stored, I obtained enough sheets to cover the walls of my compartment in exchange for drawings. At the lumberyard I found a window just right for installing between two rafters as a skylight.

Within a few days we had cleaned the attic, which was rotting after decades of neglect and covered with a thick layer of dust, dirt, and vermin. We scrubbed and disinfected the brick floors, set up the walls of the kumbals with the help of wooden frames, blankets, and sheets; we installed, out of sight, stolen electric wiring for an electric light bulb and an illegal electric hot plate. A bed frame was added with a mattress and a pillow filled with straw, a little low table, a wall shelf, and a little stool; my brand-new beloved kumbal, my private lodging, free from prying eyes.

Now I had privacy. After work I went "home" to my room. Alone, without eleven roommates with their seven women, without fights over the hot plate, without yelling, without the eternally bowing and praying engineer who only could pray in German. I could make coffee or tea substitutes whenever I felt like it, could toast slices of bread or improve my fare in other ways. And . . . I did not have to wait for the Thursday slot from 2:00–4:00 to be alone with my love in the two meter by seventy-five centimeter by seventy-five centimeter–box, to be squeezed in there and to crack one's skull when getting up. Now I was in business. I could invite a woman {to my "apartment"} properly. Due to the lack of privacy, invitations to a kumbal were very popular and sought after. And I did not have to ask to borrow {the woman's} kumbal for a few hours.

If you invited a woman, even in the ghetto, whether with or without intentions (mostly with intentions), to your private pied-à-terre (as the kumbal was called euphemistically), good manners demanded that you offered the visitor a little something, a *jause* {Austro-Hungarian equivalent of "tea"}, a supper. Without such offerings I would acquire a reputation as an uncouth bum, a shabby, stingy character.

What does a starving owner of a kumbal offer a lady? A kumbal owner, who was determined to develop an active social—or love—life, is forced to save his entertainment fare from his own rations. The raw material of such offerings (not counting the rare parcels from friends and acquaintances) consisted of ersatz coffee, bread, lentil soup (inedible even with a bouillon cube), or the thick soup made of turnips that made you feel like throwing up.

Once a week a soupspoonful of granulated sugar, once a week a piece of margarine the size of a rather thick cigarette. One slice of sausage three millimeters thick if you were lucky, or you could obtain a few cigarettes in exchange for the sugar. Thus, whenever on a late afternoon a Věruška or a Hanička comes tripping into my drawing room, everything is in readiness. The tiny table is covered with a linen napkin from home. Two people eating from the same metal canteen would be considered uncouth. A little polished wooden board will do for a serving tray. On it, crowded together, there would be the saltshaker, a jelly glass one-third or half full with sugar saved during weeks of bitter self-denial, a few slices of freshly toasted bread, two to three portions of margarine served on the cover of the canteen, and on the wall shelf a "ghetto torte." Mrs. Windholz was a champion in the preparation of this torte, which tasted almost exactly like the famous Sachertorte. The recipe was secret; its ingredients were bread, coffee, saccharine, a trace of margarine, lots of good wishes, and an electric hot plate. Very impressive and irresistible.

If there was no torte, one would serve toasted slices of bread with a paper-thin layer of margarine, sprinkled with sugar. With it we drank ersatz coffee from our own or borrowed chipped and cracked water glasses. There was no alcohol available. As a finale, to indicate one's intentions clearly, one would offer a real Memphis {brand} cigarette, followed later by a second cigarette. We never smoked cigarettes alone. We would alternate inhaling drag for drag, until {our} fingertips started to burn. Then one would carefully extinguish the stub and rub it into tobacco in the pocket. Twelve to fifteen such stubs would make a new cigarette. Who could resist such a treat?

In this manner I began a rather carefree, happy, often boisterous love life. How strange that today I can hardly remember their names and not at all their faces. I think it must be a sort of defense mechanism that keeps me from falling into deep depressions by acknowledging that most of these loving, charming creatures, these beloved women, are not alive anymore.

Two exceptions among them deserve to be talked about lovingly. Each of the two in her unique way was worthy of the truly deep affection, the all-encompassing emotion that more simply we call love. First there was Lilly (let us forget last names).

On a hot summer's day in 1943, around 6:00 P.M. after work, I was hurrying to our quarters in the Hannover barracks, going along the main square past the church. At that time of day the square was crowded like Times Square in the evening. Unexpectedly someone grabbed my arm. Before I could regain my composure, a tall, slim woman embraced and kissed me in the middle of the street saying, "Nori, thank God, at last a familiar face; don't you recognize me?" "Of course I recognize you," I stammered, hesitantly. (I had not seen her for at least ten years.) After having overcome this pleasant shock, I said, "I have forgotten your last name; I just remember 'Lilly.' Why were you sent to Terezin? After all, you have Aryan relations."

With that, she started to bawl. I tried to calm her down. We quickly went to fetch our food—lentil soup, inedible as usual—and then we sat down on a bench in the park of the Hohenelbe hospital nearby. This then is her story, which she narrated to me, interrupted by frequent bouts of inconsolable weeping.

Lilly was the only daughter of a well-known Jewish physician in Brünn. She was different. I met her frequently at the boating club and at the ballroom dancing classes when we both were very young. One could not overlook her. She was tall, a good four inches taller than I, with a wonderful athletic figure. She was an excellent skier, tennis player, and swimmer and won many competitions. Muscular but svelte, she was aware of her vitality; she had narrow hips and pleasantly rounded, firm breasts. She was totally natural, high-spirited, often bubbly, intelligent, with quick repartees. She was no bland beauty with her round face, a wide mouth, most of the time with a smile on her pink lips, a full set of dazzling white teeth, just like the ones in the Odol {brand of mouthwash} advertisement. Above the mouth a snub nose and flaring nostrils that crinkled when she laughed. The face was covered with freckles; the black, bedroom eyes were sparkling under a crown of tousled, dark-brown hair: a face that was irresistible. In addition, she was merry, bright, almost brilliant, and much too intelligent for the majority of the boys who wooed her. After completing *gymnasium* {high school}, she studied art history in Prague and had completed her doctorate.

This bright and unusually attractive creature had already had in grade school a classmate admirer, what one would call a "puppy love." She remained steadfastly faithful to him. They grew up together. He—let us call him Fritz—was a German, later called an "Aryan," from Brünn. He was from a middle-class family, later a member of the boating club, therefore a well-known comrade of us all. He was as tall as Lilly, of the same age, what one would call a good-looking boy, a well-disciplined sportsman. Nevertheless, we did not really know him. He was not shy but insincere, not open, like us; he could never smile and was morbidly jealous of Lilly, never letting her out of his sight. She was liked by everyone, but he never permitted anyone to come close.

She loved to dance; he could not prevent her from dancing with others, but after two or three minutes he would invariably cut in. Since this puppy love had almost deteriorated to the point of a monopoly, we just left the two of them alone, a fact that we all regretted. Even telephone calls {to her} were in vain. One day they got married in church with all the ceremony of a Catholic wedding, a high mass. He graduated from vocational school, a middle school, and {there} became the assistant to the instructor for mechanical engineering. She obtained her Ph.D. in art history from the Charles University in Prague. What a difference! Shortly afterward she had a child, a daughter. In those ten years I had not seen her.

On that park bench she told me tearfully what happened later. Her husband was and remained petty bourgeois; a close-mouthed, sneaky, ugly character, only concerned with promoting himself. He was not unaware of the continually spreading Nazi propaganda. The Brünn petty bourgeois, the vocational school assistant, turned into a *volksgenosse*, a Sudeten German Aryan, screaming, "*Sieg Heil, Heil Hitler*," and demonstrating for a "return to the Reich."[3]

And this true German fellow traveler became aware that his wedded wife, the love of his life, was a Jewess, a 100 percent Jewess; a Lilly "Sara" Jewish pig. She could hinder his career, his ambitious plans {to advance to} professor of the vocational school and to secretly become an SS man in the Sudeten German movement. So—divorce upon agreement, for appearance's sake. She protested vehemently, but in vain. He knew as well as she did what the divorce would mean: total abandonment of his wife, the mother of his child, loss of all civil rights of the woman, prohibition to pay alimony to the divorced wife, expulsion from the apartment, assignment into a transport. That was our friend Fritz—the reptile, the snake—as we inexperienced youngsters used to call him with uncanny instinct.

The divorce took place. Lilly managed with the help of some Czech friends to hide her daughter with some decent, {truly} patriotic Czech people in the country who promised to look after the child as if it were their own. Fritz, the Nazi, without the Jewish wife made a great career {for himself} in the SS, so great that he ended up on the blacklist of war criminals of the Czechoslovak Republic.

Of course, without protection Lilly was assigned to the next transport to Theresienstadt. I was the first acquaintance from Brünn that she had met and to whom she could pour out her heart. She managed, as the divorced wife of an SS functionary, to be protected from transports to the East. In the meantime she had grown into a mature woman of 30–32 years of age, extremely attractive. Still slim, charming, much more serious, more intelligent, irresistible. She was filled with a white-hot overwhelming hatred against her former husband, Fritz. Slowly she calmed down, knowing that her little girl was safe and well cared for. She refused to tell "the snake" where the child was hidden.

We saw each other frequently and an intimate friendship began. She worked in one of the offices in the Magdeburger barracks; later, to get a bit of fresh air, she worked in the agriculture section. In the meantime I had moved to my private kumbal.

One late afternoon after work I was sitting on my bed and sketching. I heard steps nearby, the door (the sheet-curtain) opened hesitantly, and in stepped Lilly, looking stunning, full of untamed vitality. I looked at her with amazement and before I could say anything, she burst out—how unforgettable her words have remained with me to this day—"Nori, I need a fuck—come on." She used the only honest word that however, even at that time in the ghetto, was not allowed to be mentioned.

This breathless, wonderful encounter, which I would call a passionate collision, was the beginning of a relationship full of happiness as well as of friendship; one of the exceptions that was not embittered or poisoned with the threat of separation by transport.

Lilly survived the end of the Third Reich in Theresienstadt. I met her later, as so often happened, by accident in Prague where she had been assigned to an apartment. She had her daughter with her, whom she had fetched from her friends in the country. Neither one of us had any inclination to resume the earlier relationship. Whenever I was in Prague I would visit her, a good old friend.

One day, she said, "Imagine my surprise; Fritz was here." "How come? Isn't he on the blacklist? If they catch him they will hang him." "He was here illegally, with a false passport. He said he wanted to see his child. Then he left again secretly." "I thought you hated him like no one else in the world." No answer. A few months later, Fritz came again; another few months and the apartment was empty; Lilly had disappeared. Much later I received a letter from Sweden: "We are remarried. The child is young and needs her parents. Fritz has a good job in a tool factory. I am learning Swedish and shall teach art history." Who can tell about women?

The other one was Hanička: again we do not mention last names. I have already described her. She was alone in Theresienstadt with two children, eight and ten. In spite of opportunities she had postponed her flight to safety abroad until it was too late. Her husband was in England in a secure political position.

In Brünn she lived with a woman and her nineteen-year-old son who had been assigned to the same lodgings. He was a good-looking boy but quite immature. In the course of living in such close quarters an intimate love affair developed inevitably between them. She, ten years older than the boy, was very beautiful: slender, delicate, highly intelligent, witty, and so crazy about her slavishly devoted lover that she resisted all her husband's efforts {to bring her to London} in a sort of passive way with excuses and delays. This attitude proved her undoing in the end.

I knew her slightly from Brünn. Her husband was young, perhaps in his late thirties; strong and muscular, an intelligent man, graduate of an institute for agriculture, a gentleman farmer. He had been made manager of a large estate at a very early age. The owner of the estate had died of grief over the heroic death of his only son in World War I. His widow, at the time in her fifties, was an unusually intelligent, well-preserved woman of an exceptionally strong and noble character.

After the loss of husband and son she needed a manager, estate director, and financial adviser for her large fortune. After a long search she found a bright young specialist called Freddy. He developed within a short space of time into an up-to-date, exceedingly competent estate manager and a financial manager of absolute reliability and honesty, devoted to his employer who was some twenty years older than he was. After long hesitation on her part there developed between these two doubtlessly honorable, thoughtful, valuable human beings a serious, sincere, and genuine love relationship due to their close daily contact.

The lady of the estate was a devout Catholic; her young estate manager–lover was Jewish and less religious. He was young and impetuous and insisted on marriage. This unusual lady, who loved Freddy with all the intensity of a mature woman, who had been overwhelmed by personal tragedy, refused his offer of marriage. She also was certainly aware of the difference in their ages. But how many people would have her strength of character for such loving self-denial?

She began a search for a suitable wife for her Freddy; suitable in age, religion, education, intelligence—and beauty. She found the bride; it was Hanička, the daughter of a doctor. She brought them together unobtrusively but found strong resistance on both sides. Hanička divined instinctively what the circumstances really were. Finally, the engagement took place.

The older woman gave the bride her most beautiful string of pearls as a present, which Hanička accepted very reluctantly. The older woman won over her "rival" due to her dignity, her tact, and her honest affection. The wedding took place a few months later.

Since both were Christian converts, it took place in the church, with a big wedding feast in the manor's dining room. After that the lady gave Freddy her wedding gift: the notarized transfer of the estate and a few apartment houses in Brünn to Freddy, free and clear, with only the formal stipulation to pay a yearly sum to the former owner. The old woman, a patriotic Czech, landed in Sachsenhausen where she was called "the angel of Sachsenhausen" by her fellow prisoners because of her unflagging helpfulness to her fellow sufferers.[4]

Freddy escaped to England, Hanička with the two young sons came to Theresienstadt and managed to obtain a sort of transport-protected position in the health department. She shared a small room with a lady physician in the Hohenelbe hospital. Everyone who knew her during that time knew about her affair with the boy {who was also sent to Theresienstadt and} who had no transport protection whatsoever. Thus one day, the poor woman had to watch helplessly as her loved one left irrevocably on a transport to the East. It took a few months for her to recuperate from this blow.

I visited her every so often. It must have been the summer of 1943, at a time when I still lived with eleven roommates in a room in the Hannover barracks. One day I suddenly felt ill, vomited, had unbearable pains in my stomach, fever, bouts of sweating. The "ambulance" came: a stretcher carried by two stretcher-bearers who carried me directly to the hospital in the Hohenelbe barracks. I was barely conscious, but when the examining physician's hand even came close to my lower abdomen, I would scream and jump as if electrocuted. Then came the head surgeon, called immediately by the doctor; a few more touches causing unbearable pain; "operate immediately."

The physician was Dr. Erich Springer,[5] at that time young and indefatigable, a gifted surgeon with golden hands. I was being anesthetized {while} lying helpless on the operating table. The surgical diagnosis was ileitis. The cause was the radical weight loss due to which the intestines, previously surrounded by layers of fat, were dangling around freely, and had gotten twisted into the scar tissue of previous operations, which led to ileitis. Waking up in a white hospital bed with fresh linens, I was deathly ill from the anesthetic. I was weaker than usual, miserable, the hospital smell making me want to vomit: sick, sick, sick! Nevertheless my tiny spark of determination to stay alive was still intact. This lust for life, this strength to survive, was always there.

I was lying in a large hospital room with high vaulted ceilings, one of the wards of the former garrison hospital originating from the eighteenth century. Forty to fifty other patients recently operated on shared the room with me. Having been weakened by undernourishment and the results of the surgery, I recuperated very slowly. Sick people did receive a special diet called "Reko"—soup, tea, a roll that had only half the nutritional value of the bread ration, one potato more than normal, every second day a yeast dumpling. This was prepared in the hospital kitchen. The assistant to the dietitian was Hanička. As the Reko portions, however, were, although specially prepared, small, and in my present condition I could not earn anything by selling sketches, I, that is, we, suffered from nagging hunger.

Once again I was lucky, or perhaps my guardian angel, Gabriel, intervened. Unexpectedly I received a package from Brünn. I must add that for a short period of time we were permitted to receive food packages.[6] We were allowed to send brief statements on postcards to friends and acquaintances with our address.[7] I had sent a card to my old faithful accoun-

Hohenelbe hospital ward.
(Courtesy Leo Baeck Institute)

tant, Mr. Schmid, who had informed my Czech ladyfriend, *milostpaní* (gracious lady), and my friend, patron, client, and sympathizer in general, Mr. Mojmir J., a manufacturer of hats, of the possibility of sending packages. My devoted Czech ladyfriend, a landowner, sent me a loaf of bread and potatoes. The bread arrived moldy and the potatoes rotten. I guess the love was not that great; in this case the way to a man's heart did not go through the stomach {from the German proverb: "*Liebe geht durch den Magen,*"} Bread and potatoes would have helped me during my convalescent period. Of course my brother, my two nephews, my sister Ida, and my roommates came to visit me frequently. They never came without a gift, a slab of bread, a half an apple smuggled in, a carrot.

One day, just like a deus ex machina, there came a bigger package. I must mention that all packages were "censored," that is, robbed of everything that was not normally available in the ghetto. This package, however, from Mojmir J., who had foresight and was clever, consisted of little paper bags containing barley, flour, oatmeal, dried vegetables, and some dried prunes and bread crumbs. When I emptied the flour into a glass container, there appeared a can with a soldered top with a little note on it saying "sádlo"—lard, one-half pound of it.

13

THE "PAINTERS' AFFAIR"

The Magdeburger barracks contained the nerve center of the ghetto, and the seat of the Council of Elders. It also was the office building of the Ghetto administration, its center, with the main offices of all departments, almost like the government of a state with its ministries; everything well organized.[1] The only difference was that the population governed by this administration was not counted in millions and distributed over countrysides, villages, cities, etc., with historically defined borders but that they governed a small town, surrounded by walls, moats, and fortifications with a population fluctuating somewhere between 20,000 and 60,000. The governing activities of this mini-state Ghetto Theresienstadt were under the absolute control and dictatorship of the Gestapo and SS. The orders came from Berlin via the Prague Gestapo.

I preface the following with these explanations to clarify the events described hereafter. One of the offices of the Magdeburger barracks was the graphics department, also known as the artists' group, occupying several rooms. Their task was to prepare graphic illustrations of statistics, similar to those used in annual reports of banks and industries. Reports—monthly, weekly—including every detail of conditions of health, water consumption, hospital bed occupancy, coal delivery, delivery of provisions, the expenditure of calories by age groups, and other such nonsense had to be carefully prepared and was requested with typical pigheaded German thoroughness. They had to be carefully collected in files and sent to Prague with a copy to Berlin.

The young men working in the graphics department were mostly, almost exclusively, professional artists, the majority of them from Prague. They had volunteered to go to Theresienstadt and therefore enjoyed the privilege of the AK1 and AK2. They and their immediate families were protected from transport. Some of them were my personal friends. I visited them frequently in their workrooms and in their private dwellings.

My friends were Peter Kien, a very talented young painter, Fritta, the head of the department, a more mature, serious artist, with his wife and his little boy, Thomas; the painter {Dolfi} Aussenberg from Prague; the extraordinarily mature professional graphic artist Leo Haas who had already made a name for himself as an illustrator (he and his wife were from Mährisch-Ostrau) {Moravska Ostrava, Czech city}; and the Brünn painter and professor of design {Otto} Ungar, a painter of great ability and profound concepts, a reserved man, self-contained, and a pessimist by conviction.[2]

There were also other painters in the ghetto, such as the Viennese {Friedrich} Bloch, a well-bred, friendly man, and Dr. Teichman, a physician and artist one had to take seriously as well,[3] and there were also others whose names have escaped me in the meantime, as well as some amateurs, that is, not professional painters. I count myself among the latter.

The above-mentioned painters located in the Magdeburger barracks did not merely prepare statistics for the headquarters. In their time off, evenings, nights, they sketched and painted their impressions, their criticism, their hopelessness, their despair. Of course not officially: if they would have been caught it would have meant immediate assignment into the next transport. That part of their work was hidden in safe places. We, the lesser-paid amateurs, limited ourselves to reproduce what we saw daily around us, what touched us, made us think, impressed us.

We also produced "commercially" exploitable work; for instance, I painted the bakers at their jobs to earn an extra loaf of bread, or I would paint the cooks in the institutional kitchens for some extra potatoes or an occasional yeast dumpling, and the electricians' workshop to have my simple electric hot plate repaired. Those who were not bakers or cooks were all very hungry. That half a loaf of bread meant a lot as a daily ration when you got it, together with the thin soup, ersatz coffee without sugar, and one big potato.

Oh yes, the bread: I wish I could compose a poem about the bread. The incredible taste of the bohemian black bread with its delicious dark-brown, crunchy crust. To this day I cannot resist its lure, with fresh country butter, or garlic toast with lard, or goose grease—ambrosia! . . .

The above represents merely digressions to help the reader understand the background, the atmosphere, to explain the necessity for additional income—what a joke!—where we did not even have a main source of income.

We worked eight to ten hours, six days a week, for "lodgings," plank beds, asylum, just as in a shelter for the homeless, one-half a loaf of bread, the noon soup, one or two potatoes; in the evenings, coffee without anything, sometimes the lentil soup without lentils. Additional income had to be kept very secret to guard against any possible competitors. The sources of income from the bakers and the cooks began to run dry. They had already bought their supply of sketches and watercolors and were well stocked with them. Then we found, that is, I heard by coincidence, of the great Maecenas, old Strass.[4] Old Strass, formerly a wealthy wholesale textile dealer from Náchod in Bohemia, had developed great cultural and artistic interests. We had heard that he owned a considerable collection of pictures by contemporary graphic artists. It was also said that he had a daughter married to a Czech non-Jew, and for that reason she had not been deported to the ghetto. The husband was well connected and had acquaintances among the Czech gendarmes. . . . The gendarmes had their own quarters, and their duties consisted mainly of guarding the gates leading into the Fortress Theresienstadt and supervising the schleusen procedures so that nothing would be stolen. Of course the process itself was the official looting of the luggage of new arrivals by the authorities.

The gendarmes had free access everywhere. They were correct in their official duties like professional soldiers; they were not subservient, did not carry arms, and when they felt themselves unobserved, they were friendly, sometimes even fraternizing with the Czech Jewish inmates. My nephew, Ludwig, for instance, who had served with the Pardubitzer Dragoons, had a comrade from his former squadron among the gendarmes who had served with him and who liked him and tried to be of help to him whenever he could.

The son-in-law of Mr. Strass had also found some friendly gendarmes who with great risk to themselves—surely for commensurate compensation—would smuggle contraband from the outside into the ghetto and thus supplied father Strass with food, cigarettes and, as was well known, also with money on a regular basis.

Mr. Strass, who at that time was around seventy, and his wife had been sent to the ghetto but had to live separate from one another in the barracks. It did not remain a secret for long that Mr. Strass received an abundance of all sorts of forbidden items. Nothing could be hidden; the only hiding place was under the wooden bedstead or under the pillow. Why Mr. Strass felt so absolutely secure in spite of the fact that he must have seen the continual transports to the East is hard to understand; it is possible that he had a protector high up in the hierarchy.[5]

With his liquid capital of cigarettes, preserves, margarine, bread, etc., Mr. Strass began to indulge in his former hobby again—collecting. With extreme secrecy, only known to a few artists, he bought sketches and pictures from Fritta, Haas, Ungar and also a few of my sketches. Why he had selected mine I do not know; I was, after all, only an amateur. But what I sketched was realistic as I saw it, not according to my own interpretation. My sketches, I think there were three or four, were not signed. He put them into a folder and hid them under his pillow. He paid with food that would satisfy my hunger or the yearning for a cigarette. A true Maecenas, an angel, old Strass.

None of us knew that he would add captions to the pictures. We also did not know that many—I do not know how many—pictures with the help of the same gendarmes would find their way back to Prague from where, as we found out after our liberation, they were sent on to Switzerland.[6] Supposedly they appeared there in newspapers; all that I heard only indirectly after my return. No doubt that the Gestapo got wind of this, and suddenly there were raids in the ghetto, conducted by the infamous Gestapo man from Vienna, Heindl.

The rumor was that Strass had refused to make a loan to a fellow prisoner because he was afraid that man might be an agent provocateur, which he probably was. That man sent an anonymous denunciation to head-quarters. The result was that Heindl came directly into the quarters where Strass lived with a dozen other people and systematically searched his space, and under the pillow of Strass's bed he found the folder with the sketches and with his written captions, and under his bedstead he found a suitcase with his food supplies. That is how the whole affair came to light.

Nothing much happened {at that time} except that Heindl beat up old Strass. Within minutes everyone in the ghetto knew what had happened. The wildest rumors were invented and avidly passed around by word of mouth. The folder with the sketches was sent to Berlin; there was no immediate reaction. After a few weeks the silence was broken. Measures were taken; a few SS from headquarters in Berlin appeared in Theresien-stadt.

The measures taken consisted of the painters being ordered to head-quarters, one after the other, and there, without {the SS} mistreating them, they were shown the sketches and paintings. Everyone was asked to iden-tify his own work. After that they were asked to identify the other designs according to style and technique. Almost all of them were ordered there, including Spier, the excellent, popular illustrator and political cartoonist from Holland who was a good friend of mine.

I found out from him that my two or three sketches were shown to him as well as to the others. He as well as Fritta testified that these sketches were the work of a Viennese artist whom they hardly knew and who had already left the ghetto on an earlier transport. For that reason I was not too worried. After that identification procedure it became quiet again. It seemed as if the matter had been put to rest; we dared to breathe freely again. But the Elder counselors, Edelstein and Eppstein, let us know that we should not feel too secure; they knew the SS too well. The matter might be quiet right now, but that would certainly not be the end of it.

About two months passed; we tried to forget. Then suddenly, I believe it must have been June, it was a very hot summer's day in 1944,[7] quite unexpectedly lightning struck. As I mentioned before, I was sure that I was not involved at all in the affair. I had never been called for an interrogation, and my painter friends had assured me that I need not worry. [A folder of my sketches and paintings was still under the pillow of my bed in my kumbal.] Thus I was careless—no worries for me; I was totally unprepared for the catastrophe that happened next.

I cannot remember the exact date of the day. It was around noon. I worked in my department until twelve o'clock, then I quickly went to my kumbal. . . . It was a sort of small attic room. The furniture consisted of a bed, a small table, and a wall shelf. In one corner an electric hot plate. On the bed an excelsior mattress and pillow, two woolen blankets, bed sheets dyed blue, a camouflaged electric light bulb under the mattress.

My neighbor was "Bubi" Windholz, a colleague from the technical department, and my friend. He was of slight build with a little black mustache and a slightly crooked nose; a very nice, fairly young man. He lived in a kumbal a bit bigger than mine because he had obtained permission to live together with his plump, pretty, good-natured wife. . . .

Back in the kumbal I grabbed my canteen so I could get in line at one of the central kitchens for my noon meal. Not suspecting anything, I suddenly heard my name being called, I answered to the call and there was a young man, a "runner" from the Magdeburg barracks. There was an order to appear immediately before the Council of Elders. Without my noon meal?—what was the hurry?—why immediately? I was still not too worried; perhaps it was one of the frequent requests to prepare some plans for the headquarters. But at the gate of the Magdeburger barracks another "runner" awaited us with orders to go not to the Council of Elders but directly to {SS} headquarters.

Now I began to worry a bit more, still in the vague hope that this was another special SS request. I had frequently received such special requests—orders, such as the museum space in the headquarters, or the dining and drinking hall in the SS billets. I was hoping for something like that, but my instincts were aroused and warned me: this is serious; remain calm; do not panic. I had no idea what it was about. No cigarettes, no search {of my room}. What is going on? What could have happened?

A few minutes later I arrived at the gate of the headquarters and saw the painter Ungar disappear ahead of me through a door. At the gate stood SS officer Heindl and a gendarme. Within seconds I comprehended it all: imminent danger, the painters, the next transport, perhaps "directive"— death sentence! Attention—mortal danger! Stay calm, do not panic! Difficult to do if one faces almost certain disaster.

At the gate Heindl stands silently, the gendarme asks my name and checks it off on a list. Then Heindl hauls off and hits me in the face with such force that I stagger; he bellows while kicking me, "into the cellar with you." A half-open door, a corridor, cells, another SS man, more slaps, more kicks, through another door into a semidark cellar space with a small barred window under the ceiling.

What a terrible situation! My heart sank. I was very, very depressed, but not panicky. All sorts of things pass through my mind, my whole life. I will hardly be able to keep my date with Hanička at six o'clock tonight. What will my colleagues at the office say, my neighbors, the Windholzes? Oh, my God, who will protect my sister Ida, the dear innocent, from the next transport? And I was supposed to build a kumbal for the gardeners for a salary of six apples and six cigarettes. This is the end of all of that.

The painter Ungar is sitting in a corner of the room and shaking with fits of hysterical crying. Between sobs he repeats monotonously: "We shall hang by evening. They are setting up the gallows." I am surprised at my own calm composure. But the fear is still there, makes my throat feel tight, puts a knot in my stomach. My appetite is gone, I suppress the urge to vomit.

At short intervals the door opens time and again. They enter, one after another. First the painter, Haas, then Bloch from Vienna, then Fritta, the head of the office, and then old Strass. First there is silence; then there are snatches of whispered conversations, I no longer remember about what, but I remember that they are interrupted by the crying fits and the prediction of our death by hanging monotonously repeated by Ungar. The repetitious mentioning of the gallows, which we are unable to interrupt, seems to create a pervasive feeling of depression and total hopelessness in our situation. We fall silent, everyone occupied with his own thoughts, attempting to keep our composure, to calculate our options and possibilities logically. In the corner Ungar continues with his sobbing nervous breakdown. Then whispering again, we try to guess, hopefully, what could happen.[8]

In all probability a truck will come to collect us. We imagine the road: passing the gates of the ghetto, straight to the Little Fortress. Only rumors were known about that place. It seemed to be a place without hope; they either hanged you, tortured {you}, or beat you to death. Sometimes, from the roof of the Jaeger barracks in the ghetto, one could see the pitiful, ragged, desperate shadows of the prisoners from the Little Fortress. What a horrible prospect to be one of them. If they did not hang us, how long could we survive?

The other possibility for the truck was {to go} straight then to the right at the crossing—the road to Prague. To the *Karlák*, the county court and prison in Prague, and from there a trial and deportation to another concentration camp. We hear approaching steps, the door is yanked open, and we are led, one after the other, accompanied by slaps, to interrogation. Individual interrogations, the same questions over and over again about revolutionary Communist activities in the ghetto, the customer for our pictures (Mr. Strass), organizations, clubs in the ghetto—and other such nonsense.

Then we were all together again in the cell, depressed but composed and waiting. We were prepared to be sent to the East with the next transport. Everybody was preoccupied with his thoughts: what was going to happen to the wives and the children? I thought of Hanička with her two children. What was she going to say when she heard of my arrest? We knew that everything about our fate would be known in the ghetto within minutes via "jedna bába povídala" {"through the grapevine;" literally, "an old woman said" in Czech}, the underground telegraph. How could I know in the cellar that I would never see her again? She was so sure that she had the right position, indispensable, with the necessary guardian angel and was protected from transports. What superstition! No one was absolutely protected. What good was the word of the Gestapo or the SS? Solemn promises were made to be broken. Not even the Council of Elders was secure. Of the seven members of the Council of Elders, only one, the Viennese Dr. Murmelstein, survived.

After these digressions, back to the cellar. Suddenly Fritta jumped up. Highly agitated, with tears in his eyes, he listened anxiously to a soft noise that was coming through the window near the ceiling. Then he said in a breaking voice, desperately: "I can hear Tomíček's footsteps." That was his little four-year-old boy. Then we all heard the soft steps on the street near our cellar window, then quiet again.

After about half an hour—we had lost our sense of time down there—we heard the unmistakable sound of a truck's brakes and the sound of a running motor. A few minutes later steps approach the door, the door opens, the clanging of keys; there is Heindl yelling: "Raus! Raus!" One after the other we step into the corridor and up the steps to the exit accompanied by slaps and kicks.

A few SS men are standing around. The truck stands in front of the door, covered with tarpaulin on all sides except for the back where a short ladder leads to the interior of the truck. Around the truck in a semicircle, perhaps at a distance of five meters, stand our fellow sufferers massed together, waving to us. Only a few seconds remain to me to find a familiar face. There she is, Hanička, whom I had hoped to marry after the war—what optimism—her arms raised, crying loudly, red kerchief, shining black hair. I see everything in a haze. My eyes seek to encompass the whole world that means so much to me in the seconds remaining before the truck takes us away.

"*Raus, raus*" is all we can hear now. We sit down on the floor {of the truck}. Silence. Tender words and names are spoken softly. Then we start. And now I see that Fritta was right. The families were separated in the ghetto: men's barracks, women's barracks, children's homes. Now, when it was a matter of life and death, the families were united. Waiting for Fritta in the truck was Fritta's wife and four-year-old son, Strass's wife, a frail old lady, Haas's blond young wife, Ungar's wife and daughter. Troller and Bloch were alone.

It was almost completely dark. We watched carefully. Out the gate, straight or to the right? We went straight: everybody fell silent, possibly praying. This was the way to the Little Fortress, the worst of all concentration camps. In the ghetto the horrible rumors about the Little Fortress were only mentioned in a whisper. No one who wore a Jewish star had escaped alive from there. The things happening there made the rumors and horror stories told about it seem like innocent fairy tales.

To this day I recall the months spent in the {Little Fortress} with horror and disbelief. To this day I maintain that my otherwise vivid imagination did not prepare me for the experiences there. That fortress with its unbearable terror that was concentrated on the approximately 100 Jews and an equal number of Russian prisoners was a hellish place but conceived in a hell that no one of us could possibly imagine in his wildest nightmares. In short, it was worse than what we thought hell would be like.

After a short ride, the truck stopped. We heard some guttural questions, orders to continue, a gate opened on squeaking hinges, we continued; then the truck stops. Oppressive silence reigns; then the bolts on the wooden gate of the truck are slid back; the gate falls down, two SS men open the tarp in the back: "Raus, raus," someone yells, and we climb out, one after the other, and line up, surrounded by a group of SS men who yell at us if we move ever so slightly. We have reached the first, or fourth, or fifth station, according to the individual experience of our, shall we say, "calvary." We were all sent to the Little Fortress. There we came to a parting of the ways. We did not remain in a group. Every one of us was assigned to different quarters. We lived, that is, we slept, in different casemates, underground vaults. In my casemate I was the only one from our group. We were approximately 80–100 Jews from different places in this casemate; some of them also had been in the Ghetto Theresienstadt. Every one of us learned to curse the fortress in his own way. Bloch was killed there. Fritta was mistreated so much that this man, strong as a bear, died in delirium after a few days in Auschwitz {where he was sent after his stay in the fortress}. I did not see either Haas or Ungar or their wives or children ever again in the fortress or after leaving it.[9] For this reason I can only describe the life in the Little Fortress as I experienced it by myself.

14

A CONVICT IN THE LITTLE FORTRESS

After our arrest in June 1944 in Ghetto Terezín, our group, the condemned members of the so-called "Painters' Affair," passing the Eger bridge, arrived in about fifteen minutes at the dark, dreaded gate of the Little Fortress, which was a miniature of the big fortress town, Terezín . . . Ghetto Theresienstadt; {the Little Fortress was} about one mile south of the big one. They stood on opposite ends of the stone bridge crossing the Eger River. They were supposed to protect the main road from Prussia to Prague {in Austria-Hungary} against the frequent attacks of Frederick II of

Prussia against his enemy, Empress Maria Theresa of Austria. {Later the
Little Fortress} was put to other use by the Austrian government. It was
destined as the most strictly regulated prison for long-term common and
political criminals. After the end of the Habsburg monarchy, the Czechoslovakian government kept the Little Fortress unchanged as a maximum
security prison.

{In} 1939, after the Nazis occupied the Czechoslovakian Republic, it
changed a lot. It became now the most dreaded, cruel, sadistic of all these
prisons; endless, tunnel-like, dark, dank casemate cells, laid out in twos,
facing each of four courts.

Four thousand men, Czech patriots, political "criminals," village boys
and lawyers, high officials, a minister of state, the "intelligentsia," everybody who could be a leader, and other criminals were imprisoned there.
One hundred Jews not expected to leave the fortress alive, and one hundred Russian prisoners of war shared the dreadful bunkers. The Russians
were under strict military discipline. {But} like wild {animals} they stole
everything we did not keep on our bodies. They were very strong. Every
week, some tried to escape from work, to hide in the forests, without
support {from} the population or partisans. They were caught again, tortured, then hanged and shot. Five others, innocents, were shot too, as a
warning. The Nazi executioners laughed. Days later, others escaped again,
were shot, hanged, on and on. One had to admire the courage, the heroism, of these unbending patriotic Russians.

When we were moved in July 1944 to the Little Fortress there were
rows of dark dungeons, subterranean casemates, for about 200 prisoners
each. There were heavy iron crossbars on each door and small windows
above the door. Inside was only one W.C., one dirty, slimy washstand, and
one iron coal stove with a crooked stovepipe above the window to the
court. Each {pair of} casemate entrances was connected by a vestibule to
the court. It was closed after dark by a heavy crossbarred gate. Czech

Little Fortress.
(Courtesy Leo Baeck Institute)

gendarmes opened and closed the gate every morning, {as well as} the cell doors, with huge, ancient wrought-iron padlocks with artfully wrought, monstrous keys like in Dracula's country.

Inside the casemates, which were called *zellen* {cells}, the inmates slept along both sidewalls in centuries-old bunkbeds or on the stone floor; straw mattresses, one or two blankets, two rough sheets of some kind of scratchy war material. Legions of indestructible, old-timer bedbugs and fleas shared our lodgings.

Entering the main gate, crossing a bridge over the foul-smelling moat, one felt and smelled decay, death, hopelessness, despair, and damnation. Everything was built to crush you, to leave you no hope, to convey to you your nothingness, prepare you for annihilation. You are lost!

Terezín and the Little Fortress had no railway. The nearest station where the transports from the "Hinterland" arrived and the transports to the East started was a village: Bohušovice {Bauschowitz}. . . . I already told the story of how we {unfortunate} members of the "Painters' Affair" of the ghetto were arrested and transferred to the Little Fortress. There is no hope for those who enter the Gate of Hell.

We enter. A dozen SS bark, shout, "Right! Left! Stop!" We are separated, women, children right. Women in tears, children hungry, thirsty, terribly frightened, cry. Off through some gates. We men stand for hours, unmoving in the sun, looking at the windowless, white wall. One squints over his shoulder. A sudden blow of a fist strikes him. He falls, is kicked, struggles to get up. We learn fast what we have only heard about, unbelieving. This is the Little Fortress: a name that seems so innocent, cute, almost like a toy.

Hours and hours of waiting. Then a dozen names are called. Mine and my friends' from Ghetto {Theresienstadt}. We enter, one after another, the door of the *schreibstube*, the camp office.

Two long tables, chairs, many filing cabinets, of course, the Teutonic order, efficiency. When I enter, I see a typist, red-faced, fighting single-fingered with a typewriter sitting on one side. Next to him, another higher-up with a bundle of file folders. A third one stands yawning near the door. One barks, "Answer questions quickly!"

I stand; I see a file form, printed. The one-finger typist eagerly, excitedly types: first name, last name, parents' names, race, date of birth, where, how old, schools, profession, last concentration camp, how long {there}. Some other information. The form is pulled out of the typewriter, laid flat on the table. {Someone} barks: "Sign!" {I} try to read what was written under the answered questionnaire. I am standing—impossible—too far to read. *"Abtreten!"* ("get out"). Again {we} stand in formation for hours.

Then some SS men arrive; each of them with a sheet of paper. Written on each paper are names. We are divided into groups. "Stand, do not move!" We see the SS man with our names on the paper. He is our jailer. That was the place I saw my comrades, "the artists of Terezín," {for the last time}.

The jailer's name was Stefan Rojko[1] (pronounced Roiko). He was the commander of cells on court three. A monster! He enjoyed killing people. He lusted to shoot, hang, beat, torture prisoners; to bathe his hands in blood. After six o'clock, "after work," he liked to play his violin and go for a walk with his plain, blond wife in her *dirndl* ({Austrian and Bavarian} peasant dress) and his two small children.

His background. before he enlisted in the SS police he was a lowly peasant's servant in a village in Styria, {south}eastern Austria. On the side, he was the priest's helper, the one who pulled the rope to ring the bell of the village church. He was the most rabid SS man, the most cruel, pitiless, sadistic monster of the Little Fortress except for the prison commander Heinrich Jöckl (called Pindja) and his two unattractive teenaged daughters, who, smiling or loudly laughing, never missed {the opportunity} to witness any hanging, firing squad execution, torture, or beating. The monster Rojko became Jöckl's deputy commander.[2] The others of the Gestapo, SS, kapos, were not better.

It seemed that cruelty, sadism, complete disregard of human decency, could, in the name of the Führer, be taught to eager student recruits by such dedicated, pitiless teachers as our jailers and the SS {and} Gestapo. As an example: in 1944 new Gestapo recruits were assigned to the Little Fortress; about fifteen young men, all of them volunteers (to avoid {being} shipped to the Russian front). All of them were actors from the German-speaking theaters in Bohemia and Prague, highly trained intellectuals, not a plebeian mob. One could read in their faces, the first two weeks, how honestly shocked they were seeing what was going on {in} their future theater of endeavors in the service of their God, Hitler. Could it be heredity or in the nature of their "race" that they learned so quickly? After one month of "training" they were indistinguishable from their teachers and superiors.

We newcomers too were shocked when we first saw that prisoners pushing wheelbarrows, fully loaded, did not walk; they had to run. When they broke down, their kapos beat them mercilessly with their sticks and rubber hoses. Older slave workers, after coming back from work in their quarry pits in Litoměřice,[3] deadly tired, were driven by their kapo tormentors to do calisthenics, or run five times around the court, or do fifty knee bends. Of course they could not, so the beasts, our kapos, thrashed them until they collapsed, laughing all the while. A bucket of water revived them until no bucket {of water} could help {them} anymore.

These sights were not encouraging. We could see that "Almighty God, Rojko" decided who in his cells would die and who {might} live. Rojko shouts, "Stop! Straight ahead! Take everything out of your pockets" (we are still in civilian clothes) "and leave everything on the pavement in front {of you}."

"Order! March into the kleiderkammer. Order! Strip everything!" After standing stark naked {we} walk to a shower, get a towel to dry. Another door, another wet, foul-smelling casemate. On the floor, heaps of baggy, threadbare, torn, khaki-colored uniforms, crumbling from innumerable delousing, disinfection procedures.

How well do we know these ... deplorable, unfortunate rags! {They were} the remnants of the once well-made, spotless uniforms of our army, the Czechoslovakian army, which we wore on army maneuvers with pride. {They represented} the symbolic end of a country, surrendered without a fight; a heap of khaki rags we were ordered to wear now as our new prisoner's garb. O Jerum, Jerum, Jerum {woe, woe, woe}!

Everybody tried to grab a piece. Here a cotton shirt, too long. {Underpants} too short; trousers, always too long; battle jacket, never with buttons. A cap, something undefined, two torn, gray army sheets, two cotton blankets. They left us a toothbrush, comb, and menageschale {canteen}.

Somebody barks, "Jews, step forward!" Not all of the newcomers are Jews. We are already dressed. Some other SS man with a pail of yellow oil paint stands there, a paint brush in his hand. He now paints, with the help of a stencil, a big yellow star over each Jew's heart in front and between the shoulders in the back; six-inch stars. And on the outside of our trousers a wide three-inch yellow stripe. How symbolic! We look like dismissed "yellow" generals with our trouser lampassen (the red generals' stripes) and our grand star of the "St. Israel" order, front and back. Then, finally, all procedures are over. We enter our abode for the immediate future, our cell. I have already described the damned hole.

The first man who waits for the "criminal" newcomers was a Jew. Adler was his name, our zimmerkommandant, our cell commander. Not suspecting anything wrong with another Jewish inmate, I am surprised, after the return of my fellow prisoners later, {to find} that nobody talks to him, everybody speaks in a low voice, they turn away, give no answer when he tries to start a conversation. He is totally shunned by everybody. There are about 100 Jews and 100 Russians in our cell, sometimes more. The Russians leave soon for the second of the twin cells.

I soon find out why Adler is so hated. He stayed in the cell when we went to work for ten hours daily. He stole every last crumb of bread we left hidden somewhere {as well as} the last {of the} money we were able to hide on our bodies. He reported every word we said to the damned scoundrel, Rojko. He was his spy, a shameless collaborator, an execrable subhuman species of a Jew. He tended to {have} shouting spells, his eyes bulged out of their sockets; his face was unshaven, greenish, pale skinned. When the war was over, his last victims in the cell strangled him with his own wire {noose}.

Most of my comrades, fellow prisoners, I did not know. Not all came via

Ghetto {Theresienstadt}. After all these years, they have faded in my memory. But two of them I will not forget: Dr. Wurzel from Prague and his close friend {whom} I will call "the former fat businessman from Prague" {Julius Taussig}.

Dr. Wurzel was a well-known, respected surgeon and physician in Prague; very slim, emaciated, very weak, bald, a good intellectual. He worked with us in the {mine} shafts until {he was} exhausted, chipping away with the pickax on the hard limestone, bit by bit, crouched in the dark, dripping, dank tunnels in the hill above Litoměřice. We all slaved there to convert the mile-long galleries into bomb-proof factories. Dr. Wurzel successfully cared for our medical needs with the most primitive instruments.

His assistant, the friendly, aging, "former fat man," had been in the fur business before he was placed in our cell. He was an excellent, careful assistant to our doctor. This indispensable team of genuine human beings operated on me, too.

The terrible filth of the Little Fortress and the mine shafts caused serious abscesses, inflammatory fevers starting from a little scratch, a wood splinter, {and} developing in a few hours into swollen, painful boils. After working a few hours in the shafts, a neglected splinter in my left hand developed into a messy, extremely painful abscess. I could not hold a shovel or pickax and was continually hit by our kapo. I was deadly afraid to be unable to work the next day. I {had} a high temperature. Not to work meant to be strangled by the wire noose of Rojko.

My comrades helped to get me back to our cell. Dr. Wurzel saw what happened. No anesthesia available, only some gauze and cotton, a smuggled-in gift from the kind Czech physician, some benzine to clean a wound. The doctor's main instrument was a penknife. They boiled water in a tin can to disinfect the penknife. The friendly, "former fat man," the assistant, held my arm firmly. I was shaking from fever and pain. Somebody held a dirty towel over my eyes. Then a sudden, unbearable pain as if somebody had driven a knife in my heart. The opened abscess quickly relieved the pain. Lots of blood lost, wound cleaned, some gauze, some cotton. Next morning, back to work. My team helped me to fulfill the norm {quota} of daily stone chips. I survived. God bless Dr. Wurzel and his assistant.

There was a rule stated by the camp commander, Jöckl: "{There} are no sick Jews here. Here {there} are only working or dead Jews." I was still working. {So} much {for} health care for the Jewish prisoners of the Little Fortress.

Within the fortress, no contact existed between the courts, between other cell mates. I lost track entirely of my fellow artist friends from Ghetto {Theresienstadt}. To contact anybody outside our cell was risky, dangerous, {and had to be done} furtively. Oral or written contact, when discovered, meant {loss of} your half-rations plus protracted beatings, calisthenics, etc. But {without} contact with others, with our Czech-Christian fellow prisoners, survival for us would have been increasingly difficult.

Without at least some genuine human support by our Czech fellow citizens, from whom we were not forcibly separated, our last vestige of pride, of belonging to the country where our forefathers lived for centuries, would have gone. We all knew in our hearts the separation was only temporary. Forty years of later experience convinced us it was not! {Today}, 1979 A.D., the cohesion we dreamt of has vanished.

Important for {our} everyday survival was direct, clandestine, energetic help by a few courageous, unselfish individuals; mostly simple, small-town, plain citizens. Big-city intellectuals did not help us.

The contacts between us—the "depraved," helpless, unprotected, excluded nonpersons, us Jews—and our fellow citizens, the few Christians, were infrequent. They were men of courage, not indifferent to others, willing to help us. We could only meet in passing on the autobus that picked us up at five o'clock in the morning in our courts in the fortress and drove us to work at the mine shafts of Litoměřice, about thirty miles away, and back.

The other, more dangerous way was to meet our Czech friends in dark corners of the mine shafts where we worked. We could not barter or buy anything there. What we got, thank heaven, was purely voluntary, {from} man to man, gifts from strangers. Gifts from "haves" to the "have-nots"; mainly medical supplies, aspirin, carbolic {acid}, iodine, some raisins, dried fruit.

I remember the unknown Czech miller, a small-town, social democrat, anti-Nazi, indomitable, courageous patriot. The Czechs had not many of this kind! Speaking in a low voice, encouraging {us, he said}: "We may die, but we will surely win." He put some vitamin pills and an apple in my pocket. He said, "We all have to suffer here in this damned hole. But you suffer more." We knew, we knew.

About our work? It was ghastly! Some idiots in Berlin had been informed by their German-speaking Czech collaborators and rabid Nazis of the "Sudetenland" that in the orchards of the hills around the town of Litoměřice on the Elbe River were several long-abandoned mine shafts, dug deep in the mountain centuries ago. At that time, limestone was mined to be burnt in kilns for use as lime mortar. After inspection, Berlin decided to widen the eight foot by eight foot shafts to three times the width and, where possible, to connect them to huge subterranean factory halls ten feet high as an ammunition factory. Huge, bombproof, invisible. They also filled an immense, level yard with storage halls, garages, etc., and built a brand-new road from the town up to the mine gate and a railway siding from Litoměřice to a new railway station in the orchards.

Four thousand prisoners worked on this project, slaves from the Little Fortress who were driven by bus there and back six times a week.

In a big area beneath the mountains was an immense labor camp. An eight-foot-high wire fence surrounded it. Our comrades lived strictly separated within the fences. Inside the wire fence were dozens and dozens of wooden "blocs," barracks built in regular rows on each end of the access road. . . . {Above} the fences were watchtowers manned by guards with machine guns. The . . . men working there wore a {different} crumpled garb, or uniform, than our Czech army rags. Their uniforms hung like ours on the poor emaciated skeletons like scarecrows. Only their rags were like pajamas, white and blue striped.

I {would have} to wear this garb {although I did not know it yet}, these rags, four months later. This camp was a branch, established there {in Theresienstadt}, of the monster murderous concentration camp of Auschwitz. {The victims} worked in other shafts like us and on the railway tracks. Then a couple of hundred free civilian workers, Sudeten Germans, volksgenossen, worked as specialists in the workshops, offices, and {ran the} cranes and other road machinery.[4]

The original shafts in the slopes of the orchards above Litoměřice were dug hundreds of yards deep into the mountain. {It was} solid limestone rock of a gray color. No mining had been done there for at least a century. The mouths of the horizontal shafts were closed by heavy padlocked gates. Orchard owners used some of them as cooling cellars for fruit. . . .

Slave labor, all manual, was cheap. One did not have to invest in mining machinery, compressors, batteries of drills, automated trains, etc. Slave labor was {readily} available, inexhaustible. Jews, prisoners of all occupied Slavic nations, Czechs, Poles, Russians. Machinery? Pickax and shovel, some miles of electric lighting. About 10,000 men working ten hours per day, driven to exhaustion by the kapos, to hack, in four-man teams, nut-sized chips out of the solid rock without dynamite or drilling compressors. Two men hacked, one shoveled the pieces into buckets, one man carried buckets to the {end of the line} of lorries far away, which were pushed by us in trains to the mouth of the shaft on shifting, narrow-gauge tracks.

The excavated material was piled up outside to serve as fill for yards, roadbeds, and railway dams. Even with cruelly enforced slave labor by 10,000 workers, not much hacking and filling was done. The norm for a four-man team was not more than four or five lorries of one cubic yard each per day.

The factory was never finished. With great relief, we enjoyed the daily flights of the Allied bombers and the wild scramble to pull mammoth camouflage nets, painted bright green, over the fill, to let the pilots believe they flew over the jungles of Burma. Sometimes we were driven fifty miles farther north to the large railway yards of the industrial town of Aussig {Ústí nad Labem}, in order to repair bomb-damaged railway tracks. Here we met and mingled with former Czech citizens, now Sudeten Germans called volksdeutsche. Their feelings were mixed, some influenced by old social democratic indoctrination. They still felt some loyalty to Bohemia, the country they and their ancestors had lived in peacefully for the past three or four centuries. They tried to help, in some way, when the SS was away for a beer or a nap. The younger workers were under the influence of the daily propaganda broadcast that drummed constantly into their ears: "Heim ins Reich," ("Back to the Fatherland"). These youngsters were as fanatical anti-anti-anti-Czechs, Jews, Slavs, anybody not German, as {were} the broadcasts.

The Aussig railway track work was for us unskilled slaves much harder and more exhausting than hacking in the {mine} shafts of Litoměřice. We had first to find our way through dozens of bomb craters, dirt mixed with heavy, broken stone, and everywhere bent, twisted iron rails. Even when cut in smaller pieces, it was terribly exhausting to carry heavy iron on {your} shoulders {and} with your hands; finger-cracking work.

I want to tell the gruesome story typical of the Little Fortress and its worst executioner, Rojko's, procedures. We called it then in German, "Der Watschenmann Tanz." "Watschen" means in English, "box on the ears," so it has the title "the box-on-the-ears dance."

At a certain period, about August 1944, the Jews of our cell and fifty Czechs of an "Aryan" cell worked on a job inside the fortress. There was a large court, court number four. At the end of one side was a triangular raised platform, stone paved, where they hanged and shot our brothers. The wide courtyard had thirty-foot-high walls all around. At that time every cell was already overcrowded. The high command in Prague ordered huge, new, one-story, mass cell blocks built on both sides of the yard. There we worked, carting building materials, mixing concrete, setting iron doors, scaffolding, etc. A friendly, good-hearted Czech prisoner who, before his internment, had been a building contractor in Tábor, a small town in Bohemia, planned and organized his unskilled fellow slaves, supervised, unfortunately, by our sadistic monster, Rojko, club in hand.

There was no way to hide oneself. He clubbed everybody, indiscriminately. Suddenly, I realized that he started to focus on me. I felt he looked for me. He always kicked me. A Czech boy asked permission to use the latrine. Rojko, in a rage, denied {his request} and clubbed him. The poor, sick fellow could not hold it, and all the mess went through his trousers on the concrete floor. Rojko {made} him gather the mess in a pail with his hand, but he was not allowed to stop. I saw this. Perhaps my face could still not hide my feelings. Rojko went away. I thought, I hoped, he would lay off me.

Some minutes later, he was back, with him a Czech fellow prisoner; a young, typically Czech-looking, giant peasant boy, still strong and optimistic, sunburnt, blue-eyed. What a nice, innocent, healthy boy, a typical

Hanák, {peasant from the Hana region} from a village near Olomouc, Moravia, not far from Brünn. He stopped on Rojko's side where I was still working. Rojko called me and said, "Give him a box on the ear." The boy was a full head and more taller than I, and strong! His name was Antonín. And {Rojko} showed Antonín how to slap me.

I saw Antonín almost cry, slapping me. How effectively could I slap the boy? I even had difficulties reaching his face. So we slapped and slapped (I mean he slapped). His eyes closed until I finished. Rojko, wolflike, laughed. Then Rojko hit me, kicked me, and I fainted. Some pails of water later, I came to and continued to work. On that day I knew that Rojko was "sitting" on {or had it in for} me.

Afterward, back in my cell, I drank coffee, eating my last crumb of bread just before the gendarme locked our door. Sitting on my mattress, in the darkness of the cell, suddenly a shadow; somebody sat next to me, put his hand tenderly on my cheeks, and said in a low voice: "I am Antonín from court two; forgive me, I did not want to do it. Only this German swine, Rojko." He put a piece of bread and an apple in my hand. A handshake, and the shadow, dear Antonín, vanished as catlike as he came. An unforgettable, unspoiled, good-hearted, human rock of a man, only eighteen years old. I never saw him again. I have never forgotten young Antonín, the Hanák, and hope he survived his ordeals. He did something for a fellow (Jewish) inmate, driven simply by his human decency, the goodness, the greatness of his heart, a heart as courageous as a lion's. He must have been aware of the extreme danger he exposed himself to, crossing the courts and entering another cell. Without hesitation he risked his life.

Reflecting about this period, I felt that I would have been able to stick it out, this exhausting work, if Rojko and Jöckl had not got on my back. I would work hard, I could bear a lot, and I had a strong will to survive. But after three and a half months of the Little Fortress and Rojko, I got tired; I started to lose my spirit. Sometimes I surprised myself thinking: "Is it worth it?" Fate, luck, and whatever else—I do not know—decided otherwise.

One day in September 1944 about 6:00 P.M. when we returned from work in the mine shafts of Litoměřice, as we got out of the bus, an SS man from the camp office with a sheet of paper stopped us and called out the names of perhaps a dozen of my cell mates and mine. In a concentration camp, you were always afraid to be called, singled out; one never knew. Perhaps they will execute you, or you did something you do not know {about} and they put you "*do aincliku*," in a solitary cell. We were very insecure. . . .

So we stand there, hungry, hoping we will still get our "dinner": coffee and bread. Then another SS Gestapo {man} walked out from the schreibstube, took the papers, read the names again, and said: "All inmates called by name will not go to work tomorrow, you will be "*gestellt*" {ready} in front of the kleiderkammer to exchange your garb for civilian suits. *You will leave for Auschwitz ten o'clock sharp.*"

This was news indeed. I was not afraid, hearing I would get to Auschwitz. I did not know the meaning, the implication. On the other hand, I was surprised about the change in our clothes. I never expected that somewhere they had kept the outfits in which we came. These were civilian clothes. I got my coffee and bread all right, and I did not sleep much that night.

As usual, early next morning, when the buses came to pick us up for the mine shafts in Litoměřice, I was ready with eight others from my cell. We waited inside. At seven o'clock an SS man took us outside, across a couple of now-deserted courts to the kleiderkammer. . . . Of course we did not forget to say good-bye to a few roommates we got acquainted with. Adler, the louse, tried to make friends. We treated him like dirt.

In the depot were three unknown low-ranking SS men and five Czech prisoners who worked there. Then came the SS men from the schreibstube with a list of names. We stood in single file, always ten in a row. When our names were called, we walked to a long table and stripped naked.

On the other side of the table a man gave us a bundle. They took our old rotten rags and threw them on a heap. In our bundles, when we opened them, were our old civilian clothes: everything. Surprised, we changed immediately, and we could not believe it. Some of the stuff that we had to throw on the pavement when we arrived was in the pockets. Puzzling!

When I arrived {in the fortress} in July, I only wore shorts and a shirt. Now it was September and quite cool and raining. Without a word, with only a look, one of our Czechs who worked there threw me a pair of old civilian trousers and a jacket. Again another kind, good boy of ours.

Now we could see who the released were: all civilians now, but in no way free. About fifty of us, we stood mute, unmoving, in formation. There were none of my comrades {from} the Ghetto {Theresienstadt} painters who four months {before} arrived with me. I got scared. Here were ten to twelve Jews, the others non-Jewish Czechs and much taller than we. The feared, damned kapo Spielmann from the town of Mikulov in southern Moravia, a real imbecile, {was also present}. We knew already that he killed our dear friend Bloch—a quiet, very shy painter from Vienna—with his shovel because he did not hold a pickax straight.

On the one hand I was jubilant, regardless of Auschwitz, to get away from this hellhole, the {Little} Fortress. But down in my stomach I was still fearful of the murderous hyenas, Rojko and Jöckl. I tried carefully to hide in the ranks of us fifty. At eight o'clock I heard the bus passing the gates and courts, and it stopped next to us. Shortly after, Jöckl strutted up from his quarters, whip in black-gloved hand, followed by Rojko, his deputy, holding his stick. Jöckl did not say much {except}, "You should all be shot,"—and left for the office.

Then the SS Gestapo man from the office with the file folders got out, read the names as he had done when we arrived, and again the ten or twelve of us went one after the other into the office with the long table, the one-finger typist, two SS men, but in one corner sat Jöckl. Same procedure, only that we now sat down to sign out, to confirm that they {had} returned our civilian property to us.

When I came up to sign, I sat down and could clearly read what was in front of me. I also had about five seconds to sign. Concentrating with all my brainpower alert, with all my perceptions strained, focused to grasp the content of the legal file, the "akte" as one says in German, I now signed. "Verhaftet . . . Veranworten vor dem Reichsgericht in Leipzig, nach dem Krieg. . . . Wegen Greuelpropaganda durch Verbreitung . . . gegen das Reich." In short: "N.T. {Norbert Troller} is accountable—after the war—to the highest court of the German Reich—Leipzig—for the crime he committed by distribution of horror propaganda against the Reich."

After signing this, my akte, how could I have the faintest notion that having an akte, being on file, decided my fate and saved me at our arrival in Auschwitz from transfer to the Birkenau concentration camp and being possibly selected by Mengele for the gas chambers and chimneys?[5] That I learned quickly on arrival in Auschwitz.

. . . We stood there until all was signed, all clear. Partially hidden, I saw that Rojko was looking for me. All was ready, door ajar, the motor rumbled, SS in the front seat, some in the back. "Get in!" One after another, rushing, counting, counting. Few ahead of me, more following me. I try to hide behind the half-open bus door. The man in front of me stumbles; Rojko watches, sees me, tears a crutch from under the arm of one invalid inmate and throws it like a javelin at my head. He misses, and it crashes into the door. I, full of fear that he may pull me out at the last second, slip like a fish under a seat.

The bus starts, far too slow, crosses the courts, a short stop at the dark Gate to Hell, straight ahead, left turn, and away on the main road to Prague. Temporarily saved! Breathing again, hoping again, you damned, crazy, wretched bunch of murderers, Rojko and Jöckl.

NOTES

INTRODUCTION

1. Raul Hilberg, *The Destruction of the European Jews*, 2d ed., 3 vols. (New York: Holmes and Meier, 1985).

2. See Yehuda Bauer, *They Chose Life: Jewish Resistance in the Holocaust* (New York: American Jewish Committee and Jerusalem Institute for Contemporary Jewry, 1973); Yuri Suhl, *They Who Fought Back* (New York: Schocken Books, 1978); Isaiah Trunk, *Jewish Responses to Nazi Persecution: Collective and Individual Behavior in Extremes* (New York: Stein and Day, 1979).

3. We are indebted to Dr. Sybil Milton for her notes and comments clarifying the chronology of events in Theresienstadt and other details concerning its history. Her suggestions for amending the Introduction and source notes have been particularly valuable.

4. Several public hangings took place in Theresienstadt in early 1942 in which sixteen people were executed for such "crimes" as smoking and smuggling out letters. H. G. Adler, *Theresienstadt, 1941–45* (Tübingen: J. C. B. Mohr, 1960), pp. 86–88. Subsequently, all murders and tortures of the inmates for violation of rules were carried out in the *Kleine Festung* (Little Fortress), a small fort outside the camp in which criminals were also housed. It was in this fortress that Norbert Troller was incarcerated before being sent off to Auschwitz after he was found to have surreptitiously drawn pictures of the true living conditions in Theresienstadt.

5. Ibid., p. 157.

6. Franz Hvass, "Besog i Theresienstadt den 23 Juni, 1944" (Visit to Theresienstadt, June 23, 1944), in H. G. Adler, *Die verheimlichte Wahrheit: Theresienstadter Dokumente* (The hidden truth: Documents of Theresienstadt) (Tübingen: J. C. B. Mohr, 1958), p. 752. A similarly laudatory passage is cited in Arthur R. Butz's notorious book, *The Hoax of the Twentieth Century* (Torrance, Calif.: Historical Review Press, 1976), pp. 144–45, in order to support his thesis that the Holocaust never happened. Butz audaciously concludes: "What the Red Cross saw at Theresienstadt was part of regular SS policy" (p. 145). In fact, Dr. Hvass "had purposely reported conditions more favorable than he had found them in order to encourage the Germans to allow the Danes to continue shipments of foodstuffs and medical supplies to the camp." Harold Flender, *Rescue in Denmark* (New York: Simon and Schuster, 1963), p. 222. Flender admits, however, that the Danes' report was "glowing" (p. 222).

7. Susan Cernyak-Spatz, "Theresienstadt: A False Front and Its Heroic Reality," paper presented at the North Carolina Humanities Conference, Statesville, N.C., November 1984.

8. Biographical information is from the catalog, *Terezín 1942–1945 through the Eyes of Norbert Troller* (New York: Yeshiva University Museum, 1981).

9. Troller typed MS, pp. 170–71. The pagination refers to a segment of the manuscript written originally in English by Troller but not included in this edition of the memoir. A copy of this portion of the manuscript can be obtained at the Leo Baeck Institute in New York, N.Y. It is cataloged under "Troller Manuscripts." Most subsequent references to the Troller manuscripts will refer to the holograph copy in Troller's own hand, which is also designated as "Troller Manuscripts" in the Leo Baeck Institute.

CHAPTER ONE

1. In 1938 and 1939, 117,000 Austrian Jews emigrated to other countries. Yehuda Bauer, *A History of the Holocaust* (New York: Franklin Watts, 1972), p. 109. The difficulty of emigrating to other countries is exemplified by the restrictions imposed by the U.S. "quotas." Only 27,000 immigrants from Germany and Austria and 6,500 from Poland were permitted to enter the United States yearly prior to World War II. Raul Hilberg, *The Destruction of the European Jews*, 2d ed., 3 vols. (New York: Holmes and Meier, 1985), 3:1112–13.

2. Approximately 185,000 Jews remained in Greater Germany in September

1939, 60,000 in Austria, and 100,000 in Bohemia and Moravia, the "Protectorate," as the Germans called it. Henry Friedlander, "The Deportation of German Jews–Post-War German Trials of Nazi Criminals," *Leo Baeck Institute Yearbook* 29 (1984): 208. Although, according to Hilberg, there were approximately 60,000 surviving Jews on German soil at the end of the war, they included displaced persons from Poland, the Netherlands, France, and other countries. *Destruction of the European Jews* 3:1048. The actual number of surviving German-speaking Jews, however, was minuscule. As an example, Friedlander writes that out of 35,000 Berlin Jews deported to the East—not including those who were sent to Theresienstadt—only 20 returned from Łódź, none from Kovno, 31 from Riga, 11 from Reval, 7 from Minsk, 1 from Lublin, and 178 from Auschwitz. All the rest were murdered in the camps. "Deportation of German Jews," p. 217 n. 72.

3. According to Doris Rauch, Troller is probably referring to a Czech couple named Miskevic whose country house he built.

4. *Kanada* was the term used in Auschwitz to indicate the warehouse in which confiscated clothing and other possessions were stored to be sent back to Germany for local use. Troller could not have known the term until after he arrived there. *Schleuse* (channel) was Nazi jargon for the process of confiscating possessions used in Theresienstadt. (Cernyak-Spatz) According to Rauch, officially, all valuables were confiscated by the Nazis before deportation.

CHAPTER TWO

1. Nisko was an experimental camp set up in October 1939 for the Jews who were deported from Ostrava and Vienna. It was located on the San River near Lublin in Poland. The plan, however, did not work, and the camp at Nisko was dissolved in April 1940. Zdenek Lederer, *Ghetto Theresienstadt* (New York: Howard Fertig, 1983), p. 12.

2. "Dora" is Doris Rauch, presently of Washington, D.C. Troller erred in his recollections since the "child," Dora, was twenty-one years old at the time of her deportation. From December 2, 1941, to April 8, 1942, nine transports with 8,923 Jews left Brünn for Theresienstadt. Only 325 of the Jews were still alive in the ghetto by July 1944. Ibid., table 4, p. 252.

3. Approximately 150,000 Jews were murdered in Estonian territory. Aharon Weiss, "Categories of Camps—Their Character and Role in the Execution of

the 'Final Solution of the Jewish Question,'" in *The Nazi Concentration Camps* (Jerusalem: Yad Vashem, 1985), pp. 126–29.

4. The term "racial shame" was established as a result of a German racist law in 1935 that, among other things, voided any marriage and illegalized any extramarital relations between Jews and "citizens of German or kindred blood." Raul Hilberg, *The Destruction of the European Jews*, 2d ed., 3 vols. (New York: Holmes and Meier, 1985), 1:159.

5. Gustav Böhm (1885–1974) was a Czech painter who worked in France. According to Rauch, he was in France at the time that Troller lived in his home.

6. The *Zeile* (Cejl in Czech) was a long and ugly street leading from the Municipal Theater to the suburbs of Zábrdovice (Obrowitz). According to Rauch, the Trollers, ironically, had their fur business adjacent to the Zeile across from the Municipal Theater as well as a hat factory at the back of 53 Zeile where the family lived. Troller was forced to move from there when residential restrictions were imposed on Jews in Brünn.

7. The Little Fortress housed political prisoners. It was here that one of the heads of the Council of Elders, Dr. Paul Eppstein, was murdered by the Nazis on September 27, 1944. H. G. Adler, *Theresienstadt, 1941–45* (Tübingen: J. C. B. Mohr, 1960), p. 188.

CHAPTER THREE

1. Troller MS, p. 256.
2. Troller MS, p. 244.
3. Troller MS, p. 244.
4. Troller MS, p. 246. According to the map of Theresienstadt, there were seven streets running horizontally and nine vertically. Zdenek Lederer, *Ghetto Theresienstadt* (New York: Howard Fertig, 1983), pp. 244–45.
5. Troller MS, pp. 246–47.
6. Troller MS, p. 247.
7. Troller MS, p. 247.
8. Troller MS, p. 245.
9. Troller MS, p. 248.
10. Troller MS, p. 176.
11. AK1 and AK2, the *aufbaukommando* (construction detail), were the first

transports of young Czech Jewish males who arrived in Theresienstadt on November 24 and December 4, 1941. They helped to build the ghetto. Lederer, *Ghetto Theresienstadt*, p. 14.

12. Troller MS, pp. 241–42.

13. Troller MS, p. 195.

14. In September 1942, the ghetto inhabitants numbered 56,717, the highest monthly figure. Lederer, *Ghetto Theresienstadt*, p. 46. By the end of 1944, however, due to disease as well as deportations, the population had been reduced to 11,000 (p. 263).

15. Troller MS, p. 250.

16. According to Rauch, not until the town was evacuated of civilians in June 1942 were Jews allowed to leave the barracks without a permit.

17. Despite the promises of the Nazis, only 44 of the original 1,300 men from the AK1 and AK2 transports were still alive in Theresienstadt on July 11, 1944. Lederer, *Ghetto Theresienstadt*, table 4, p. 252. Of the 141,184 people sent to Theresienstadt, 88,202 were deported to "the East," 33,456 died in the ghetto, 1,654 were released prior to liberation, 464 fled, 276 were arrested and probably killed by the Gestapo, and 16,832 survived in the camp. Raul Hilberg, *The Destruction of the European Jews*, 2d ed., 3 vols. (New York: Holmes and Meier, 1985), 2:438. Lederer's figures differ slightly.

18. Troller MS, p. 225.

19. Troller was on one of four transports that left Brünn for Theresienstadt on March 19, 23, 29, and 31, 1942. Of the 4,000 Czech Jews sent in these transports, only 124 were still in the ghetto by July 1944. Lederer, *Ghetto Theresienstadt*, table 4, p. 251.

20. Otto Zucker was a member of the *Ältestenrat* (Council of Elders) as a "first substitute" (or alternate). He was a Zionist, a patron of the musicians in the ghetto, and himself a violinist. He died in September 1944, presumably in Auschwitz. Julius Gruenberger, a Zionist as well, is less favorably described as a typical bureaucrat, a sensualist, obstinate, vain, brazen, and "humorless." He also is presumed to have died in Auschwitz in the spring of 1944. H. G. Adler, *Theresienstadt, 1941–45* (Tübingen: J. C. B. Mohr, 1960), p. 248.

21. Erich Kohn is cited by Adler as one of the members of the "staff." He is reputed to have been one of the officials who knew as early as February 1943 that the fate of the deportees to "the East" would be the gas chambers. Ibid., p. 735.

22. The monthly mortality rate recorded by Adler bears this out. From De-

cember 1941 through March 1942, the number of deaths recorded in the ghetto was 237. In the next three months it almost tripled (683); in July alone it reached 983, in August 2,357, and in September there were 3,941 deaths. During this period, it should be noted, the average age of those who died was between 70 and 75. Ibid., p. 523.

23. Troller MS, p. 251.

24. Some 17,000 urns of the ashes of victims (not "hundreds of thousands") who died in the ghetto were thrown into the Eger, but in October 1944, much earlier than Troller seems to indicate. Lederer, Ghetto Theresienstadt, p. 158.

25. In March 1945, shortly before the second Red Cross inspection, the Nazis ordered the surrender of all documents and statistics of the period prior to January 1, 1945, which were in the possession of the Jewish Administration; these records of Nazi atrocities were promptly burned. Ibid., p. 178.

26. In fact, disease played a very significant part in increasing the mortality rate in Theresienstadt. Between 1942 and 1944, over 8,000 people died of enteritis, over 6,000 from pneumonia and other infectious respiratory diseases, and 2,000 from general "infections." Adler, Theresienstadt, p. 528. The most serious disease, however, was typhus. In February 1943, the peak of the first epidemic of this disease, there were over 400 cases. At the time of liberation, in April 1945, however, there were over 1,300 cases (p. 515). Over 500 of these victims died. In all, a total of 18,000 of the inmates died of infectious diseases in Theresienstadt. Lederer, Ghetto Theresienstadt, p. 264.

27. Troller MS, p. 251.

CHAPTER FOUR

1. From January 1942 until October 1944, 63 transports were sent from Theresienstadt to the East. Of the almost 87,000 victims sent off, less than 3,000 survived. In April 1942, shortly after Troller's arrival, no less than 7 of these transports, each consisting of 1,000 victims, were sent to the East from Theresienstadt. Of this group, barely 40 survived. Zdenek Lederer, Ghetto Theresienstadt (New York: Howard Fertig, 1983), table 3, pp. 250–51. For slightly different figures, see Raul Hilberg, The Destruction of the European Jews, 2d ed., 3 vols. (New York: Holmes and Meier, 1985), 2:438.

2. According to Rauch, Troller's chronology of events was incorrect. Alice and her daughter were not transported to the East until September 1942, more

than six months after his arrival. He may have confused their permanent deportation with their shipment to Křivoklat—a town near Theresienstadt—on "temporary duty" to plant trees. H. G. Adler notes that 1,002 men and women were sent there for that purpose on April 10, 1942. *Theresienstadt, 1941–45* (Tübingen: J. C. B. Mohr, 1960), p. 834.

3. Ernst Möhs was a high-ranking SS official in charge of the "Final Solution" at Oranienburg. He was Eichmann's assistant in overseeing Theresienstadt. Ibid., p. 141.

4. In October 1944 they were taken to Auschwitz and immediately sent to the gas chamber; Rabbi Leo Baeck also survived. Lederer, *Ghetto Theresienstadt*, p. 157.

5. Since the initial number of AK1 and AK2 commandos was far less than Troller's figures, the number of "protected" was actually much smaller. Moreover, as previously noted, few of these "privileged" inmates actually survived.

6. Fritta (a.k.a. Fritz Taussig) (1907–44) was one of the most prominent of the artists to depict surreptitiously the life of the ghetto through drawings and paintings that were smuggled out of Theresienstadt and actually survived the Holocaust. Adler, *Theresienstadt*, p. 614. Along with Fritta, Otto Ungar (1897–1945), and Peter Kien (1919–44), Troller was among the artists caught by the Nazis and sent to Auschwitz.

CHAPTER FIVE

1. Raffael Schächter, a young conductor, actually directed a production of Smetana's *The Bartered Bride*, which was performed in the ghetto on November 28, 1942. The production was such a success that the work was performed thirty-five times. H. G. Adler, *Theresienstadt, 1941–45* (Tübingen: J. C. B. Mohr, 1960), p. 593. This achievement gives an insight into the rich cultural and intellectual activities engaged in by the ghetto inhabitants of Theresienstadt despite the harshness of living conditions and the continual threat of deportation.

2. Leo Baeck (1874–1956) was one of the most prominent leaders of the Jewish community and head of the Jewish Federation (*Reichsvereinigung*) in Berlin before he was sent to Theresienstadt in January 1943. Raul Hilberg, *The Destruction of the European Jews*, 2d ed., 3 vols. (New York: Holmes and Meier, 1985), 2:448. He was the deputy to the head of the ghetto and the chairman of

the Council of Elders as well as director of the welfare department. Adler, *Theresienstadt*, p. 197.

CHAPTER SIX

1. Troller MS, p. 165.

2. The *berušky* were not Jewish women but Germans under the authority of the SS. H. G. Adler, *Theresienstadt, 1941–45* (Tübingen: J. C. B. Mohr, 1960), p. 142. They were not the women who officiated in sorting the belongings at the schleuse. They made raids into the women's quarters to find contraband but would end up stealing anything they could get their hands on. The word *berušky* comes from the Czech word *brati*, meaning "to take or steal."

CHAPTER SEVEN

1. Troller was briefly married before the war.

2. Dr. Karl Bass is noted for his involvement in the health care in Theresienstadt rather than his activities in the Ghetto Guard. H. G. Adler, *Theresienstadt, 1941–45* (Tübingen: J. C. B. Mohr, 1960), pp. 98, 523.

3. The figure in question was Karl Loewenstein who had been a high-ranking German officer in World War I and aide-de-camp to the German crown prince. He was actually appointed the head of the Ghetto Guard in September 1942 and created a sort of "Praetorian Guard" from this group. He was in frequent conflict with the Ältestenrat because of his high-handedness in giving his Guard special privileges. He was eventually replaced in September 1943 when the Germans discovered what he was doing. Zdenek Lederer, *Ghetto Theresienstadt* (New York: Howard Fertig, 1983), pp. 59–60. Adler, *Theresienstadt*, pp. 138–39.

4. Loewenstein was actually half-Jewish. Adler, *Theresienstadt*, p. 138.

CHAPTER EIGHT

1. Cleanliness was a very important element in keeping up the morale of the inmates in this and other camps, especially when conditions were difficult for

maintaining good hygiene. When I was in Auschwitz, one of the first signs I noticed of emotional disintegration among the inmates was when they did not try actively to keep themselves clean. (Cernyak-Spatz)

2. Dolfi Aussenberg, a native of Prague, was another well-known artist who was part of the group caught in the "Painters' Affair." He was barely a year older than Peter Kien, who was only twenty-two when he entered the camp. H. G. Adler, Theresienstadt, 1941–45 (Tübingen: J. C. B. Mohr, 1960), p. 616.

3. As alluded to before, the cultural life of Theresienstadt was extraordinarily rich. Concerts, lectures, and opera and play performances were frequent. In addition to The Bartered Bride, such operas as Carmen, Tosca, and The Magic Flute were performed, as well as plays by Shaw, Hofmannsthal, Molière, Gogol, and Shakespeare. Ibid., p. 590.

4. The prominente were the so-called "privileged" members of the ghetto including well-known figures in the arts, sciences, and education; military leaders; and prominent members of pre-Nazi society. They were originally brought to Theresienstadt in the fall of 1942. Ibid., p. 310.

5. In January 1943, there were 127 cases of typhus, increasing to 414 in February and then subsiding rapidly to 150 in March and a negligible number by June. Ibid., p. 515.

6. "On August 17, 1938, Ministerialrat Globke, the 'name expert' in the Ministry of the Interior, issued a decree which required that Jewish men had to add the name 'Israel' as a middle name, and 'Sara' for a woman. Other 'approved' names included Faleg, Feibisch, Feisel for males ... and Scharne, Scheindel, Scheine, Schewa ... for females ... as well as many other distortions and figments of the imagination." Raul Hilberg, The Destruction of the European Jews, 2d ed., 3 vols. (New York: Holmes and Meier, 1985), 1:176. Such "Germanized" names as David, Michael, Eva, and Ruth were not included. The name changes had to be reflected in birth and marriage certificates. Ibid.

7. The elaborate steps taken by the Nazis to create the impression that there was a ghetto bank involved creating over 50,000 personal accounts for which monthly statements were made of "deposits" and "charges" in the worthless currency issued in the camp. The banking system even included mechanized bookkeeping and fifty to sixty people to keep the "accounts." Dr. Desider Friedmann, the last president of the Vienna Jewish Community, was the head of the bank. Ludwig Hift, "The Bank of the Jewish Self-Government Administration in Terezín," in Terezín, edited by Frantisek Ehrmann (Prague: Council of Jewish Communities in the Czech Lands, 1965), pp. 165–66. Friedmann was

appointed a member of the Council of Elders on November 24, 1942. Adler, Theresienstadt, p. 115.

8. "The few hundred persons who in the period from the middle of May to the middle of August 1945 had the luck to report as returned camp inmates could, after identification, receive a sum between 1,000 and 5,000 crowns, as did those who remained in the camp, too." Hift, "The Bank," p. 16.

CHAPTER NINE

1. Actually, the numbers involved were much smaller—several thousand. H. G. Adler, *Theresienstadt, 1941–45* (Tübingen: J. C. B. Mohr, 1960), p. 408.

2. Of the approximately 7,000 children (fifteen years old and under) who at one time or another passed through Theresienstadt, about 6,300 were murdered in the east. Ibid., p. 573.

3. Troller is being ironic. There was one miserable little "café" in the ghetto but, of course, no movie houses.

4. This is an allusion to the German proverb: "*In der Not frisst der Teufel Fliegen*" (in an emergency the Devil eats flies).

CHAPTER ELEVEN

1. Troller is referring to the "Embellishment" that took place the following year when the Red Cross was invited to Theresienstadt and visited on June 23, 1944, to see a "model" camp for the Jews, which was, in fact, a total fabrication.

2. Siegfried Seidl became the first commandant of Theresienstadt in December 1941. He was a brutal man who ordered the executions of the sixteen men who were hanged early in 1942 and also ordered beatings for minor infractions such as smoking. He was replaced in June 1943 by Anton Burger on Adolf Eichmann's orders because he could not adapt to the public relations plans for the ghetto. Zdenek Lederer, *Ghetto Theresienstadt* (New York: Howard Fertig, 1983), pp. 21, 90.

3. Actually, according to Lederer, Burger's rank was major or sturmbahnführer, although that promotion might have occurred later. His cruelty, as Troller reports, was known by the Czech Jews of Brünn when in 1940 he rounded up 200 of them from the streets and sent them to Mauthausen, endorsing their

files with the initials "R.U.," *rückkehr unerwünscht* ("return undesirable"). Ibid., p. 75. One survivor actually reported that Burger personally assisted in torturing prisoners (p. 79).

4. Spier worked on the film the Nazis used as propaganda to show to the Red Cross during their visit in 1944. H. G. Adler, *Theresienstadt, 1941–45* (Tübingen: J. C. B. Mohr, 1960), pp. 182, 184.

CHAPTER TWELVE

1. On October 5, 1943, eighty-three Danes were sent to Theresienstadt. Another four transports brought a total of 466 Danes to the camp. Zdenek Lederer, *Ghetto Theresienstadt* (New York: Howard Fertig, 1983), table 5, p. 262. It was due to the efforts of the Danish and Swedish Red Cross that these Danes were given better treatment than most of the other inmates because shortly after their arrival these organizations insisted that they be permitted to inspect the conditions in which their countrymen lived. Ibid., p. 100. This request became the impetus for the "Embellishment."

2. A few months after the visit of the Red Cross on June 23, 1944, mass transports to the East, which had stopped just prior to the visit, resumed. From October 1 to October 28, eleven transports containing over 18,000 inmates were sent to Auschwitz from Theresienstadt. Of those, barely 1,500 of the victims survived. Ibid., table 3, p. 251.

3. Among the Czechs were quite a number of German-speaking nationalists who welcomed the annexation of the Sudetenland in 1938. The 1930 census lists over 2,200,000 Germans in Bohemia out of a population of 7,000,000. Radomir Luza, *The Transfer of the Sudeten Germans* (London: Routledge and Kegan Paul, 1964), p. 1.

4. Sachsenhausen was an all-male concentration camp until the last year of the war.

5. Springer became the head of surgery for the camp on December 4, 1941, and in the fall of 1944 became the head of the hospital in the EVl section of the camp. H. G. Adler, *Theresienstadt, 1941–45* (Tübingen: J. C. B. Mohr, 1960), pp. 817–18.

6. From October 1942 the first packages from outside reached Theresienstadt. Of course, most of these packages were "inspected" and plundered before they reached their intended recipients. Ibid., pp. 576–77. Eva Noack-

Mosse in her unpublished memoirs of Theresienstadt records lists of packages that were sent by the Red Cross to the inmates and were never distributed. One such list noted 200 crates of packages, each of the 4,000 packages consisting of one kilo of sugar, one can of vegetable soup, one rabbit paté, and one package of cookies. Eva Noack-Mosse MS, Leo Baeck Institute, New York, N.Y.

7. Noack-Mosse states that in February 1945 the postcards were limited to thirty words and could only be sent out once every two months. The cards were, of course, censored by the SS before mailing. Noack-Mosse MS.

CHAPTER THIRTEEN

1. Zdenek Lederer, *Ghetto Theresienstadt* (New York: Howard Fertig, 1983), devotes an entire chapter to the organizational plan and administration of the ghetto (pp. 57–87). Over 17,000 people worked in the ghetto bureaucracy in nine major departments including welfare, health, and labor. H. G. Adler, *Theresienstadt, 1941–45* (Tübingen: J. C. B. Mohr, 1960), p. 394.

2. Ungar had taught at the Jewish secondary school in Brünn before the war and managed to survive his incarceration when he was deported from Theresienstadt to Auschwitz but died of typhus in a sanitarium on July 25, 1945. "Who's Who," in *Terezín*, edited by Frantisek Ehrmann (Prague: Council of Jewish Communities in the Czech Lands, 1965), p. 325. Kien's drawing survived although he died with his parents in Auschwitz. Ibid., p. 320. Haas (1901–83), a painter who worked in Vienna, not only managed to survive the war but enjoyed a career as a graphic artist for television and film in East Germany after 1955. Ibid., p. 319. He wrote his own memoirs of the "Painters' Affair" in which he refers to Troller a number of times. Leo Haas, "The Affair of the Painters of Terezin," in *Terezín*, pp. 156–61. Aussenberg is only given brief mention by Adler. *Theresienstadt*, p. 616.

3. There is only one reference to Bloch in Adler; he noted that Bloch's drawings survived to be exhibited at Yad-Vashem in Jerusalem, January–March 1960. *Theresienstadt*, p. 834. There is no mention of Teichman.

4. There is no mention of Strass in Adler, and he is only briefly alluded to by Lederer. *Ghetto Theresienstadt*, p. 120. His full name was Frantisek Strass, a department-store owner who had Gentile family connections and was, therefore, given some special privileges. Gerald Green, *The Artists of Terezin* (New York:

Schocken Books, 1978), p. 98. His role as a "collector" of the pictures that brought on the undoing of the painters is described in Troller's narrative.

5. Haas mentions two brothers named Přikryl, who served as contacts among the Czech gendarmerie, but he did not seem to know of any higher-ups who might have protected Strass. "Affair of the Painters," p. 158.

6. Although Troller may not have known, Haas certainly did. In fact, according to Haas's memoir, his motivation, and that of a number of the artists, was precisely the hope that their pictures would be seen by the outside world to reveal what the Nazis were really doing. This smuggling had gone on for two years before it was finally discovered. Ibid.

7. Both Troller and Haas indicate that the arrests occurred in June; the latter placed it on June 17, but since the arrests occurred after the Red Cross visit on June 23, the date of July 17 in Lederer, *Ghetto Theresienstadt*, p. 120, is undoubtedly more accurate.

8. Haas's report of the incident is more complete concerning interrogations of the suspects. Eichmann himself officiated. What Troller did not know was that the reason the arrests were finally made was that the Red Cross was suspicious of the "show" they were presented on their visit to the camp in June, and the Nazis suspected that one of the reasons for the Red Cross's skepticism was that they had seen some of the drawings and paintings that depicted life in the ghetto as it really was. Haas, "Affair of the Painters," pp. 158–59. Strangely, Haas does not mention the earlier interrogation noted by Troller in his memoir, but he does add that the painters took great care to conceal their work, going so far as to wall in many of the drawings in one of their rooms. Ibid., p. 158.

9. Ungar died of typhus, as already noted, and his wife and daughter survived; but Troller recounts in another part of his memoir that he knew of Haas's survival. Troller typed MS, p. 168. In fact, Troller and Haas visited Fritta in the infirmary in Auschwitz. Green, *Artists*, p. 122.

CHAPTER FOURTEEN

1. According to notes and news clippings provided by Troller, Rojko concealed his identity after the war but was arrested in January 1946 in the Ober Landsberg Camp where former SS members were kept. He was tried in September 1951 and freed on a technicality; but he was retried in 1962 in Graz for fifty-four murders and given a life sentence.

2. Jöckl is cited in Lederer as being implicated in the concealment of the murder of Dr. Paul Eppstein, the second leader of the Council of Elders. Zdenek Lederer, *Ghetto Theresienstadt* (New York: Howard Fertig, 1983), p. 151. It was Jöckl who, in late 1944, along with Rahm and Möhs, ordered the disposal of the ashes of some 17,000 victims of Theresienstadt by scattering them into the Eger River. Ibid., p. 158. According to Troller's notes, Jöckl was tried and hanged in Litoměřice along with two other SS officers, Neuwirth and Schmid, by a "people's court" shortly after the war.

3. The quarry to which Troller refers, now and subsequently, was a limestone quarry northwest of Litoměřice under the Bidnice Hill where in 1944 the Nazis decided to develop an underground factory. Three to five hundred prisoners from the Little Fortress were among those used in performing the preliminary work for the factory. Many were Yugoslavs who had been brought in March 1944 from Dachau and were temporarily stationed in the Little Fortress. In May inmates of the Flossenbürg concentration camp were also used. The camp of the Flossenbürg inmates at Litoměřice was called the Richard Camp, the largest branch of the Flossenbürg in Czech territory. The factory was built for the Auto Union (armament) and Osram (electrical) concerns and was under the direction of SS *Gruppenführer* (Lieutenant General) Kammler, the head of Technical Construction, Group C, in Himmler's *Wirschaftsverwaltungshauptamt* (SS Economic and Administrative Office). The project was actually of no value to the German war economy and was merely used as a way of hastening the prisoners' deaths. In the work commando to which Troller may have been assigned, there were 1,506 men including 73 Czechs of which only 20 were Jews. On May 9, 1945, the entire Nazi staff fled, and on May 10 the Red Army freed 17,000–20,000 prisoners. This information was made available through the unpublished records of the Svaz protifašistickych bojovniku (Union of Anti-fascist Fighters) in Prague, which were translated from the Czech by Barbara Podoski. A published source confirming this information is *Terezín*, edited by Milan Balcar (Ústí nad Labem, 1988), pp. 276–77.

4. Troller mistakenly assumed that his fellow prisoners were from Auschwitz when they were actually from Flossenbürg.

5. Auschwitz was a concentration camp; Birkenau was the "sister" death camp, which used slave labor as well as immediately executing the sick, the elderly, and children. Auschwitz III, the slave-labor camp, was also known as Buna-Monowitz.

GLOSSARY

Ältestenrat. Council of Elders. The governing body of the Jewish community set up and controlled by the Nazis in the ghettos throughout the territories under their domination.

"Arbeit macht frei." "Work liberates." The Nazi slogan used in all the camps and ghettos to give the Jews the illusion that if they cooperated with the Nazis by working for them, they would not be harmed.

Aufbaukommando. Construction detail, abbreviated AK1 and AK2. This term designated the first two transports of Jews who set up the facilities for the inmates of Ghetto Theresienstadt.

"Auf weisung." "As directed." Nazi euphemism written on some prisoners' records for their immediate execution by shooting or gassing upon arrival at a concentration or death camp.

Bauhof. The lumberyard at Ghetto Theresienstadt. The inmates constructed their own beds and simple furniture as well as filling special orders for the Nazi command there.

Berušky. German women under the authority of the SS who ostensibly raided the women's quarters in Ghetto Theresienstadt in order to find contraband but ended up stealing whatever possessions of value they could find. The term is derived from the Czech word "brati," meaning "to steal."

Blockwart. Block warden. The Nazi official at the grass roots level in German towns and cities. He spied on people and made sure that official orders affecting the general community were carried out.

Buchteln. A Czech yeast-dough pastry.

"*Der Führer schenkt den Juden eine Stadt.*" "The Führer Grants a City to the Jews." The title of a propaganda movie made by the Nazis to show the outside world that the Jews were being well treated in Ghetto Theresienstadt.

Dirndl. An Austrian and Bavarian peasant dress.

Gruppenführer. SS term for lieutenant general.

Gymnasium. European secondary school. Completion of the coursework would be considered the equivalent of the first two years of college in the United States.

Hanák. A peasant from the Hana region of Czechoslovakia.

"Heim ins Reich." "Back to the Fatherland." A propaganda slogan of the Sudeten Germans who supported the "repatriation" of the German-speaking areas of Czechoslovakia into the Reich.

Hochschule. College or university.

Jause. An Austro-Hungarian afternoon repast somewhat similar to "tea" in Britain.

Judenältester. The head of the Council of Elders. See Ältestenrat.

Judenrein. Literally, "Jew-free." The Nazi policy of eliminating the Jews of Europe first by deportation and then extermination.

Kaiser-und-Königliches gelb. Literally, "imperial and royal yellow." A shade of yellow identified with official residences of the Austro-Hungarian Empire.

Kameradschaftsheim. The living quarters of the SS garrison at Ghetto Theresienstadt.

Kanada. A term used in Auschwitz to designate the storehouse for all of the confiscated belongings of the Jews.

Kapo. An inmate used by the Nazis as an overseer of his fellow prisoners. Rarely was a kapo Jewish.

Karlák. The county court and prison in Prague.

Kleiderkammer. The clothing depot in any camp.

Kleine Festung. The Little Fortress. It was here that political prisoners and criminals were incarcerated just outside the walls of Ghetto Theresienstadt. The Jewish prisoners that the Nazis intended to murder for political offenses were also kept here.

Kolatschen. A Czech yeast-dough pastry.

Kommandatur. The SS headquarters in Ghetto Theresienstadt.

K.u.K. Abbreviation meaning "imperial and royal." See Kaiser-und-Königliches gelb.

Kumbal. Czech for "cubbyhole." Private rooms built into the nooks and corners of the living quarters in Ghetto Theresienstadt.

Lampassen. The red stripes on a general's pants. Austro-Hungarian military term.

Menageschale. An army canteen for food and drink.

Meshuggenah. Yiddish for "crazy people."

Milostpani. Literally, "gracious lady." A polite Czech term for a woman.

Obersturmführer. SS term for first lieutenant.

Penezeln. Thin pieces of toasted bread with garlic on top.

Pied-à-terre. A small apartment for an assignation.

Prominenten. A Nazi term given to the Jews who, because of their former eminence in the community or political connections, were given "special" treatment in Ghetto Theresienstadt. They were assigned better quarters than the other inmates, but otherwise their treatment was much the same as everyone else's.

Protektorat. The Nazi term for occupied Czechoslovakia.

Rassenschande. Miscegenation. Literally, "racial shame." Nazi term for violation of the Nuremberg Laws concerning the prohibition of any sexual or social contact between Jews and Aryans.

Rathaus. Town hall.

Reichsvereinigung. A general term for a federation of religious, ethnic, or professional groups in the Third Reich.

Rückkehr unerwünscht. "Return undesirable." A Nazi euphemism for an execution order written on a prisoner's file. Abbreviated as "R.U."

Sachertorte. A delicacy made with chocolate and filled with jam. The recipe originated at the Hotel Sacher in Vienna.

Schammes. A minor official in a synagogue. The equivalent of a beadle.

Schleuse. Literally, "channel" or "funnel." The area through which the Jews were registered and systematically robbed (*schleusen*) of their possessions upon entering Ghetto Theresienstadt. *Geschleust* became an expression for taking something that was not yours: it was the equivalent to "liberating" in military slang.

Schreibstube. An administrative office or orderly room in the military.

Šlupky. Czech word for potato peelings.

Sturmbannführer. SS term for a major.

Tallith. A Jewish prayer shawl.

Volksdeutsche. A term for Sudeten Germans. Many of them demanded annexation of the Sudeten area of Czechoslovakia into the Reich prior to 1938.

Volksgenosse. "Racial" and party comrade.

Watschen. A slap in the face.

Wirtschaftsverwaltungshauptamt. SS Economic and Administrative Office.

Wrucken. Austro-Hungarian word for turnips.

Zellen. Prison cells.

Zimmerkommandant. The prisoner responsible for the administration of a room or cell of inmates.

INDEX

Illustrations are indicated by page numbers in italics.

Adler (prison spy), 149, 157
AK1 and AK2: construction detail, 24, 26, 31, 80, 93, 118; protection of, 37, 39, 132; special quarters, 111
Antonin (prisoner), 155–56
Auschwitz, xx, xxvi, xxxiii, 42, 49, 59, 60, 61, 86, 92, 153, 157, 158
Aussenberg, Dolfi, 60, 100
Aussig, 154

Baeck, Rabbi Leo, 47
Bass, Dr. Franz, 64, 66, 67
Bauschowitz (Bohušovice), 17, 20, 47, 55, 146
Berušky, 58, 63
Bloch, Friedrich, 132, 139–42, 158
Böhm, Gustav, 11
Brünn (Brno), xxvi, xxix, xxxi, 2, 4, 8, 10, 11, 12, 15, 26, 28, 36, 40, 42, 64, 66, 69, 90, 98, 115, 122, 123, 124, 125, 126, 128, 132, 156
Bunzl-Federn, Hanne, xxvii, 61, 68
Bunzl-Federn, Ida, xxvii, 39, 44, 50–51, 61, 62, 68, 107, 130, 138
Bunzl-Federn, Julius, xxviii–xxix, 55, 61–62, 68
Bunzl-Federn, Marianne, xxvii, 46, 53
Burger, Anton, xxv, 115–16

Cigarettes, 77, 80, 121; smuggling, 38–39; value of, 94, 112
Council of Elders, xxxii, 23, 24, 26, 27, 31, 35, 37, 65, 68, 78, 93, 103, 131, 135, 140; deciding on transport lists, 35, 40, 47–51; and "protection," 36; housing privileges, 42, 43, 111–13
Czech gendarmes, 22, 39, 58, 63,

134–35, 144–45
Czechoslovakia, xxi, 2, 10, 17, 82, 141; army, 148

Danish prisoners, 87, 118
Diseases: diarrhea, 53, 62; typhus, 83, 86, 88
Dresdner barracks, 23, 24, 27, 44, 74, 76, 112

East, the, 39, 50, 65, 69; disappearance in, 9, 17; Theresienstadt as a transit station to, 27; transport to, 28, 33, 34, 38, 46, 49, 56, 87, 90, 92, 108, 113, 118, 127, 135
Edelstein, Jakob, xxv, 37, 49, 51, 136
Eger River, 30, 105; bridge, 17, 21
Eichmann, Adolf, xxv, 35, 47, 50
"Embellishment," the, xxiv, xxv, xxvi
Eppstein, Paul, xxv, 49, 136

"Fritta" (a.k.a. Bedrich Taussig), xxxiii, 41, 78, 132, 135, 136, 139, 142

Gestapo, 3, 24, 26, 37, 38, 58, 132, 147, 157, 159; and the "Painters' Affair," 135–40
Ghetto bank, 59, 87
Ghetto Guard, 55, 63, 65, 78
Gruenberger, Julius, 28, 30, 37, 39, 49, 51, 112
Gutmann, Dr. Helena, 100

Haas, Leo, xxxiii, 132, 135, 139, 142; wife of, 132, 141
Hamburger barracks, 23, 25, 27, 44, 76

Hannover barracks, 23, 25, 80, 96, 100, 118, 121
Heindl, Rudolf, 135, 136, 138, 140
Hohenelbe barracks, 25, 86, 137
Hohenelbe hospital, 122, 128, 129
Hohenelbe park, 48, 122

Jaeger barracks, 27, 47, 55–56, 139
Jöckl, Heinrich, 147, 151, 156, 158, 160

Kanada, 5, 6, 59
Kapos, xxxiii, 147, 148, 150
Kavalier barracks, 23
Kien, Peter, 78, 132
Kohn, Erich (Era), 28, 31, 36, 37, 51, 80, 96, 118; and "protection," 40–41. See also "Protection," concept of
Kumbal(s), 38, 43, 44, 96, 99, 113, 114, 119–20, 124

Leitmeritz (Litoměřice), 104, 148, 157; forced labor in the mine shafts of, 150, 152–54
Little Fortress, xxxiii, 19, 21, 62, 105, 108, 139, 141, 142, 143, 144, 145, 146, 150, 156, 158
Loewenstein, Dr. Karl, 65–67

Magdeburger barracks, 23, 25, 35, 42, 51, 78, 79, 80, 113, 131–32, 133, 137
Maloměřice, 4, 11
Maria-Theresa, Empress, xxi, 17, 72, 83, 147
Möhs, Ernst, 37, 47, 50
Murmelstein, Benjamin, 36, 112, 140

Nazis, xix–xxii, xxiv–xxv, xxx, xxxi, 2, 5, 8, 12, 17, 22, 25, 28, 69, 91, 144, 152

"Painters' Affair," the, xxxiii, 51, 78, 131–42, 143, 146
Pardubitzer Dragoons, 10, 63, 134
Perlhafter, Alice, xxvii, xxix–xxx, 8–10, 27, 34, 39, 61, 69, 92
Perlhafter, Dora (Doris Rauch), xxvii, xxix–xxx, 8–10, 34, 39, 61, 69, 92
Prominente, xxi, 83, 87, 118
"Protection," concept of, xxxii, 32, 33–45, 48, 50, 51, 68, 110, 113, 118, 127

Red Cross Commission, 41, 59, 113
Rojko, Stefan, 147, 148, 150, 155–56, 158–60
Russian prisoners, 144, 149

Sari (Troller's housekeeper), 11–12, 27, 34, 92
Schächter, Raffael, 47
"Schleuse(n)," 55–56, 57, 58–59
Seidl, Dr. Siegfried, 115
Spier, Jo, 116, 136
Springer, Dr. Erich, 128
SS (storm troopers), 30, 41, 49, 53, 67, 106, 118, 123, 138, 140, 146, 154; control of Council of Elders, 37, 40, 47, 51–52, 53; greed of, 38–39, 58; investigation of the "Painters' Affair," 136; arrest Troller, 138; release Troller, 157–59. See also Jöckl, Heinrich; Little Fortress; Rojko, Stefan

Strass, Frantisek, 134–36, 139–41
Sudeten barracks, 25, 27, 30, 41, 71, 72, 76, 78, 96
Sudeten Germans, 123, 153–54
Sudetenland, 152

Theresienstadt (Terezin), 33, 34, 36, 40, 68, 69, 86, 90, 92, 102, 104, 107, 108, 109, 125, 127, 134, 136, 143, 146, 150, 158; as transit station, 2; arrival of Troller family in, 9, 60–62; entering the camp, 17, 19, 21; resettlement of Jews in, 25–26; initial organization of, 37; transports, 46; and the "schleuse," 55–56; engineering department at, 80; gender ratio in, 90; social classes in, 93; and Gestapo, 132
Transports, 3, 27, 62, 64, 80, 82, 93, 95, 110, 113, 115, 124, 135, 138, 146. See also "Protection," concept of
Troller, Ernst, xxvii, 10, 12, 27, 55, 60, 63, 67
Troller, Fritz, 10, 67
Troller, George, xiv, xxvii, 2, 60, 69
Troller, Grete, 10
Troller, Hans, 11, 60, 67
Troller, Herbert, xiv, xxvii, 60, 69
Troller, Karl, xxvii, 2, 60, 69
Troller, Ludwig, 10, 17, 55, 63–67, 69, 134
Troller, Norbert: life of, xxvi–xxvii; reluctance to write, 3, 7, 51, 62–63; hiding places for valuables, 5–6; farewells to family members, 8–9, 11, 62, 69; deportation of, 11–13,

15–16; arrival in Theresienstadt, 17, 26; meets officials, 27–28; work in the technical department, 30; loss of weight, 94; change of quarters, 96–118; illnesses, 99–100, 127–28
—commissions: of kumbals, 42–43; of view of Theresienstadt, 103; of SS quarters, 115
—life in the Little Fortress, 143–60; forced labor at Litoměřice, 150–54; forced labor on the Aussig railway track, 154; torture, 155–56; extradition to Auschwitz, 157–60
—love life: "Hanička," 98–99, 126–27, 138–41; "Lilly," 121–25
—"Painters' Affair," the: participants sell sketches, 135; arrests and torture, 138; participants sent to Little Fortress, 139–42
—protection: of self, 34, 40–41; of sister Ida, 50–51; of nephew Ludwig, 66
Troller, Paul, xxxiii, 3
Troller, Stella, 10–11, 55, 66–67
Troller, Vilma, 2, 60, 69

Ungar, Otto, 132, 135, 138–39, 141–42

Windholz, "Bubi," 101, 102, 137, 138
Windholz, Kathie, xxxiv, 120
Wurzel, Dr., 150–51

Zucker, Otto, 27, 30, 37, 39, 42, 43, 49, 51, 66

Made in the USA
Middletown, DE
30 March 2024